THE WILD WEST

This edition published in 2008 by Usborne Publishing Ltd,
Usborne House, 83-85 Saffron Hill,
London EC1N 8RT, England.
www.usborne.com

Printed in Great Britain

Edited by Jane Chisholm
Designed by Brenda Cole
Series designer: Mary Cartwright
Cover design by Michael Hill

USBORNE TRUE STORIES

THE WILD WEST

HENRY BROOK

Illustrated by Ian McNee

CONTENTS

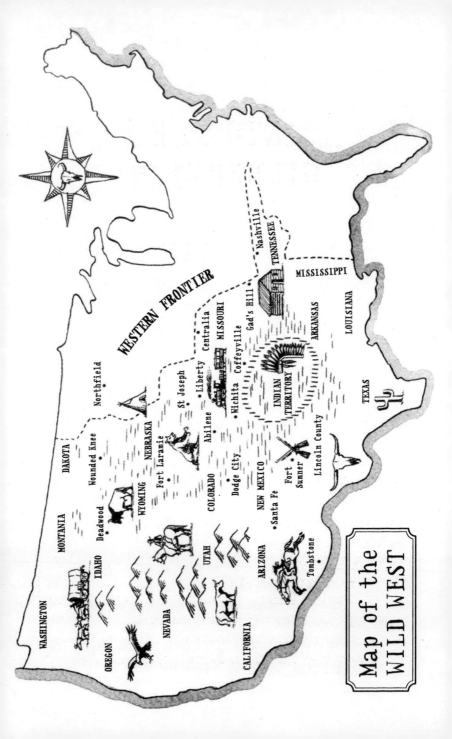

Map of the
WILD WEST

INTO THE WILDERNESS

"It was a land of vast silent spaces, of lonely rivers, of plains where the wild game stared at the passing horseman, of scattered ranches, of long-horned cattle, and of reckless riders who unmoved looked into the eyes of life or death."

Theodore Roosevelt, An Autobiography

When the first European settlers landed in America in the 1600s they discovered a pristine wilderness of great rivers, mountains and forests. They cleared the trees to build their homes and plant their crops, often relying on handouts of food from friendly tribes of Native Americans. The settlers built farms and schools and churches. When they needed more space, they just pushed deeper and deeper into the woods and began fighting with the same tribes who had helped them when they first settled there.

The Native Americans had lived as wandering nomads in these forests for thousands of years. They moved their own villages with the changing seasons and barely marked the earth with their comings and goings. They couldn't understand how the settlers thought anyone could actually own the land. But the Europeans put up fences around their farms and claimed the land was theirs.

This was the frontier, the place where the West began – these little farms and towns jutting into the wilderness. For over 200 years, the frontier moved west across the country's vast prairies, mountains and deserts, following the drift of America's swelling population. Trappers and "mountain men" pushed west as they hunted for valuable animal skins. Gold strikes in Colorado and California attracted prospectors from around the world, and settlers streamed out to the fertile valleys of Oregon, drawn by the promise of free land.

In a time before railways or roads, families and explorers crossed America in wagons, by horse and on foot. Their route took them through the treacherous passes of the Rocky Mountains and across a treeless country of open plains and sun-baked earth as wide as an ocean. These high plains east of the Rocky Mountains were known at the time as the Great American Desert. Thousands died in this desolate landscape, from disease, hunger and thirst. Others were murdered by bandits or hostile tribes. But still the wagons kept on coming. The frontier moved along behind them as towns and cities grew up on the grasslands, steadily taming the wilderness.

The unexplored, western territory was a magnet for anyone who wanted to leave his or her past behind, start again and perhaps get rich in the process. It was the newspaper writer John Soule who first coined the phrase, "Go West, young man," in a rallying call to adventure-hungry people in the eastern cities. And millions came.

Over forty frenzied years of expansion and development, they laid telegraph wires and railway tracks to link the country's coasts, built great cities, levelled forests and dammed the rivers. By 1900, the wilderness was gone – and so was the frontier. But the idea of the Wild West, and the memory of the heroes and villains who lived there, still hold a special place in our imaginations.

The cowboy, gunslinger, saloon gambler and town sheriff are familiar characters to us all and we can recognize their human qualities and faults within our own, modern communities.

Like the warrior knight of the Middle Ages, the humble cowboy stands as one of the most romantic figures in history. Fighting to survive and uphold their way of life on the fringes of civilization, the people of the Wild West have provided us with a set of enduring and amazing true stories.

THE MOUNTAIN MAN

"We were then in a dangerous, helpless situation, exposed daily to perils and death amongst savages and wild beasts..."

Daniel Boone, frontier explorer

Hugh Glass stepped through a wall of bushes into a clearing and noticed two bear cubs playing in the long grass. A second later he saw the mother bear charging towards him to defend her young. She was a full-grown grizzly, the strongest and most dangerous animal in North America. Glass had a choice to make – and quickly. He could either run – or try to kill the bear with a shot from his rifle.

Glass was a veteran mountain man, one of thousands of fur trappers, hunters and explorers who spent their lives wandering deep into the wild forests and plains of the western frontier in the early 1800s. He knew a lot about bears. A grizzly could outrun a horse over a short distance and kill it with a single swipe of its powerful paws. Its teeth could crack through bones and its claws were as long as a man's hand and sharp as razors.

The Mountain Man

There was little chance of outpacing a grizzly but some people still ran, looking for a tree to climb. Mountain men joked that there were only two types of tree in the forest: ones you could climb and ones you couldn't. But Glass knew that a grizzly could rear up on its hind legs, reaching high into the air. The bear might scoop him out of a tree before he could escape it. Glass lifted his rifle and took aim.

He only had time for one shot. The bear was just yards away, snarling and spitting as it bounded towards him. Glass pulled the trigger, hoping to strike a weak spot in the thick layers of fur, fat and muscle that protected the grizzly's body. The bear stumbled as the shot ripped into its skin, but it kept on coming.

Glass dropped his rifle and ran, reaching for two pistols in his belt as the grizzly slammed into him, knocking him over. It fixed its teeth into his shoulder and shook him like a doll, while Glass fired his guns into its belly. Screaming in pain, Glass dropped his pistols and sank a knife into the bear's neck. The bear slashed at him with its claws, ripping open the flesh across his back, scalp, legs and ribs and tearing a hole in his neck. Glass stabbed again and the bear howled and fell dead across his mangled body.

In the early days of the Wild West, the land was full of hazards and only the toughest characters survived to make their mark on the frontier. Glass was hiking across the rough country that is now South Dakota when he was mauled by the bear.

It was 1823 and he was a scout and trapper for an expedition led by Major Andrew Henry up the Missouri River, one of 100 men who had volunteered to leave civilization behind them for a few years in pursuit of riches. There were fortunes to be made, dealing in animal furs, and Glass was helping to find new trapping grounds and set up forts and trading posts for Henry's fur company.

Glass was an independent, stubborn man by all accounts. He had been foraging for plums on the day he was attacked, disobeying his employer's strict orders not to wander off alone into the woods. Henry's expedition was already a year old and there were barely a dozen volunteers left from his original force. He was leading them to the safety of a distant post – Fort Henry – but he'd lost 12 men just a few days earlier when Arikara warriors attacked their camp. Glass had been shot in the leg during the attack, and there were warriors still lurking in the woods hunting for the explorers.

But Glass was used to a dangerous life. And, besides, he was hungry and nothing would deter him from collecting some juicy fruits.

Hugh Glass was born in Pennsylvania in around 1780 and his adventures began as a young man when he was kidnapped by pirates and press-ganged into their crew. After two years at sea, Glass escaped with a sailor, swimming from their pirate ship to the Texas shore. They tramped all the way to Kansas, but Pawnee warriors captured the pair before they could reach a friendly settlement.

The Pawnees killed the sailor, but Glass found a packet of *vermillion* – bright red dye – in one of his pockets and offered it to the chief. Vermillion was precious to the Pawnees, who used it to paint their skin in times of war, and the chief spared his life. Glass stayed with the tribe for several years before he became a trapper, learning their secrets of how to hunt and live off the land. This wilderness training would prove essential in the weeks after the bear attack.

When the other members of the expedition reached Glass they rolled the dead grizzly away and gasped at the sight of the wounded man. Glass had been nearly torn to pieces and blood was bubbling out of the hole in his neck each time he sucked for air.

Henry and the other men had mixed feelings about their bleeding comrade. They were furious with Glass for leaving the safety of the group and worried that the noise of the shots he had fired would betray their position to the Arikaras. But it was their duty to care for the injured man, stitch his wounds and wait with him until he died. None of the expedition thought Glass would survive until nightfall and Henry made plans to bury the mountain man under some rocks before leaving camp in the morning.

Dawn came and Glass was still breathing. Henry couldn't risk waiting in this dangerous country for another hour, so he loaded the wounded man onto a stretcher made of broken branches roped together. The trappers took turns dragging or carrying Glass through the woods and over rocky terrain, while the unconscious man groaned and coughed at every jolt.

But, incredibly, after five or six days of this torture, Glass was still alive. His wounds were festering and he seemed weaker than ever, but he was clinging onto life. Henry stopped his men by a stream and explained to them that the stretcher was slowing them down, risking all their lives. He asked for two volunteers to stay with Glass until he died. Nobody stepped forward. Next, Henry offered a reward of $80 to anyone who would wait with Glass at the stream. Two trappers accepted the job: a man named John Fitzgerald and a teenage boy named Jim Bridger.

The Mountain Man

For four days, Bridger and Fitzgerald sat with Glass, listening to the eerie silence of the woods and keeping their eyes peeled for warriors. Each morning they checked their patient for signs of life, and each morning his condition was the same. His skin and hair were caked with blood and he couldn't talk or open his eyes – but Glass was alive. Bridger and Fitzgerald knew that the nearest doctor was hundreds of miles from their hiding place in the woods. There was no hope for Glass and the two men knew that with each passing day their friends were getting further ahead of them. It also meant that the warriors had a greater chance of finding their camp.

On the fifth day they rolled Glass into a shallow grave and covered him with a bearskin and a layer of twigs and leaves. They took his guns, his knife and the last of his food, and marched away, safe in the knowledge that Glass was sure to die soon and their awful crime would never be discovered.

Bridger and Fitzgerald had underestimated the mountain man. Days after he was abandoned, some spark of life flickered inside Hugh Glass and he opened his eyes. He dragged himself out of the grave and drank from the stream. Although he was injured, alone and unarmed in the wilderness, Glass didn't panic or give in to despair. He picked and ate some berries from a bush and rested his body. When he woke again, a snake was lying coiled on the ground beside his head. Glass dispatched it with a stone, skinned it with a razor he found in his pocket and ate it raw, mashed up with more berries to improve the taste.

After a few days of eating fruit and drinking from the stream, Glass was strong enough to crawl a few yards. The bear had snapped his leg, so he reset it himself, binding the limb with some sticks and twine. His wounds were infected and wriggling with maggots but at least they had stopped bleeding.

After examining himself, he decided he was strong enough to set out along the banks of the river in the direction of Fort Kiowa. It was a brave plan. Glass would be crawling on his elbows and knees and his destination was over 500 km (300 miles) downstream. But he had a powerful motive to keep him going: he was burning with revenge for the men who had stolen his belongings and left him for dead.

Crawling a few hundred yards each day, Glass survived on the roots, berries and grasses that he'd learned were safe to eat when he lived with the Pawnee. If he came across the rotting carcass of a dead animal he split its bones with rocks and sucked at the marrow inside. One morning he spotted some wolves, gnawing at a freshly killed buffalo. Glass waited until the wolves had eaten their fill and moved off, then stole some fresh meat from them. After gorging on the buffalo he decided he was now strong enough to walk. With the aid of a strong stick, he started to cover three or four miles a day.

His first encounter with other human beings – after

almost two months completely alone in the forest – was with a party of friendly Sioux warriors. Glass had learned enough sign language to communicate with the tribe and he quickly told them his tale. The warriors applauded him for his bravery in grappling with a bear. Then they treated his wounds and put him across a horse for the last leg of his journey and the ragged, bloodstained mountain man finally arrived at Fort Kiowa in October.

Castaways and wilderness survivors usually spend a few weeks or months resting and healing after their ordeal, but Glass had grit and he only stayed at the fort long enough to sleep, eat and buy stores and weapons for another trek. He left for Fort Henry on a riverboat, vowing to chase Fitzgerald and Bridger to the ends of the Earth.

It took him over two months to locate Major Henry and his men, after a journey just as arduous as his march to Fort Kiowa. He arrived at their camp during a New Year's Eve party and when Glass stepped into the room the tipsy Bridger thought a ghost had come to haunt him. He turned white and trembled with terror, until Glass took pity on the boy. Instead of pumping Bridger with bullets, Glass gave him a public scolding and declared that because Fitzgerald was the older man he would bear sole responsibility for their crime.

Fitzgerald must have been tipped off about the mountain man's return from the dead and his quest for revenge. The trapper had deserted from Henry's camp a few months earlier and drifted south to Fort Atkinson, Nebraska. It took Glass almost six months to reach the fort. By then his quarry was safe from any assault. Fitzgerald had enlisted in the army and the fort's commander warned Glass that it would be unwise – and unhealthy – to shoot a man in uniform.

Glass had to settle for a formal interview with Fitzgerald in the commander's office, but he still gave the new soldier a piece of his mind. He ended by demanding the return of his rifle and Fitzgerald obliged before shuffling away in disgrace. He must have been mocked and chided by his peers in the regiment because they raised $300 as a gift for Glass before the old trapper left the fort.

People like Glass lived a wild life in a wild country. Solitary, self-reliant and strong, they had a close relationship with the land. Their wilderness skills of trapping, hunting and trading with the Native American tribes made them heroes to many of the people who followed them out to the frontier.

Over time, their legendary adventures were overshadowed and replaced in the popular imagination by tales of the scouts who rode out onto the plains. The scouts gave way to the lawmen, and cowboys and men-with-no-name gunslingers finally took their place in a thousand Western movies. All these Wild West figures had something in common. They were tough, they could live off the land and they expected to be treated fairly, and as equals, by their fellow man. Hugh Glass lived by these rules.

He died in the wilderness fighting Arikara warriors, less than ten years after his battle with the bear.

PRINCE OF THE PISTOLEERS

"Wild Bill with his own hands has killed hundreds of men. Of that I haven't a doubt. 'He shoots to kill,' as they say on the border."

Colonel George Ward Nichols, journalist

Nobody knows for certain when the army scout, gambler and gunfighter, James Butler Hickok earned the name that would become part of Western legend – Wild Bill. Whispers, lies and fantastic stories always swirled around the man, and some parts of his life have vanished forever into the dust and shadows of frontier history. Most people believe he picked up his title after a showdown in the town of Independence, Missouri, in the early 1860s.

He was already using the name Bill, or Dutch Bill – perhaps in memory of his father, William – and was out walking in the town when he spotted a crowd dragging a frightened bartender from a saloon. A gang of cowboys were shouting for someone to fetch a hanging rope. There had been a fight in the saloon and the bartender had shot and wounded one of their friends. Bill didn't like the look of the cowboys and he thought the accused man deserved a proper trial – so he pushed his way through the throng. When he reached the terrified bartender, he wrestled him away from the cowboys and blocked their path, gripping a revolver in each hand.

The people in that crowd were no strangers to guns and many of them were armed. Men carried weapons for protection and almost out of habit in that rough country. But the citizens of Independence were farmers, cowhands and shopkeepers. They saw something rare and dangerous in Bill's eyes, something that made them hesitate to draw their own guns. Bill was a veteran gunslinger – cool, calm and ready to kill. Nobody was lynched in Independence that day.

A woman at the edge of the crowd suddenly called out: "Well, look at him, he's a wild one."

And the name stuck.

Wild Bill was born on the frontier, in a small, wooden framed house in the village of Homer, Illinois. His parents had moved west to open a general store for settlers, but in the year of his birth – 1837 – a banking crisis rocked the nation. The Hickok store went out of business and the family turned to farming. Wild Bill spent his early years on the edge of the wilderness, roaming the lonely woods, clearings and open prairies that stretched far to the distant horizons.

From an early age, guns fascinated him. He was still a boy when he bought his first pistol, after saving all the pennies he could earn doing farm work. Wild Bill quickly taught himself how to shoot by stalking game for the family pot. When he wasn't hunting in the woods, he shot at targets to improve his aim, or spent hours trying to master drawing and balancing his guns with both hands. He kept to a routine of daily shooting practice for most of his life and loved to demonstrate his skills to weapons enthusiasts and journalists.

It was a newspaper writer who later gave him the name "Prince of the Pistoleers" and other journalists swore that Wild Bill could shoot the cork out of a bottle without breaking the glass, or blast a hole through a spinning coin. Experienced gunslingers must have chuckled when they heard these fantastic stories, but nobody doubted that Wild Bill was a "shootist" – an expert with a gun. He always claimed that nobody would ever kill him in a face-to-face fight and his grim boast turned out to be true.

The young farm boy with a passion for guns grew into a handsome risk-taker who always paid uncommon attention to his appearance. Even in the roughest mining camps and dustiest frontier towns, Wild Bill would go hunting for soap and a tub of hot water. He wore his hair long, in a mane of auburn curls that fell down to his shoulders, and dressed his six-foot frame in a wide-brimmed sombrero, dapper buckskins and fine leather boots.

Instead of using a common holster on each hip for his two Colt revolvers, he tucked the guns into a belt or silk sash tied around his waist. When he stopped in a town, he spent his days in the saloon, gambling at the card tables or swapping yarns at the bar. Wild Bill stood out from the crowd, and he loved to amaze both friends and strangers with tales of his exploits. To visitors from the eastern cities he was the very picture of a frontier hero – charming, fearless and larger than life. But it would be wrong to dismiss Wild Bill as a saloon boaster. In his short life he witnessed or played a part in many of the major events and changes that shaped the West.

Wild Bill's first brush with danger came when he left home at nineteen, looking to start his own farm in former Indian Territory (the name given to the Native American lands) west of Missouri. Despite treaties promising them permanent rights to this region, Native American tribes had been forced off their traditional hunting grounds to make way for white settlers in a new American state: Kansas.

Tens of thousands of settlers were lured to Kansas by the offer of cheap land. But the birth of the state was bloody and violent, as rival groups battled over whether the territory should join the southern states in supporting slavery. Wild Bill stepped into a war between anti-slavery "Free-Staters" from the North, and so-called "Border-Ruffians" from the slave-owning state of Missouri. Gangs of riders from both sides prowled the countryside, burning houses and plundering the farms of their enemies.

The Hickok family had helped to smuggle runaway slaves to freedom back in Illinois and Wild Bill's sympathies lay with the Free-Staters. By day he earned his living as a farmer, but at night he rode with anti-slavery vigilantes – civilians who used force to protect their communities and beliefs. Wild Bill's skill with a gun didn't go unnoticed and he was invited to join the bodyguard of a prominent Free-Stater. It was around this time that he was escorting a wagon train and saw a young boy being thrashed by a bully. Wild Bill rescued the child and the two became friends. The boy's name was William Cody, but he was better known in later years as the frontier daredevil and showman, Buffalo Bill.

The fight for "Bleeding Kansas" (as it became known) gave Wild Bill a taste for adventure that he couldn't satisfy being trapped on a farm. When the Free-Staters won a key vote ensuring that slavery wouldn't be tolerated in Kansas, he took a job with a stagecoach company. It was dangerous work, guiding teams of horses across the desolate, prairie trails and guarding shipments of gold, money and mail from attacks by road agents (another name for bandits).

Wild Bill's luck ran out early in 1861, when he was injured in a stagecoach crash and his employers sent him to recuperate at an isolated ranch at Rock Creek, Nebraska. This lonely collection of cabins, a barn and a corral (a pen for cattle or horses) was the scene of a gunfight that earned Wild Bill his lifelong reputation as a dangerous man with a gun.

Rock Creek was a Pony Express station, one of more

than a hundred stations linking Missouri with California. In the days before a telegraph line or railway crossed America's vast interior, it could take weeks for stagecoaches to deliver the important mail between the gold fields around San Francisco and the financial powerhouse of New York.

The Pony Express used a relay system of individual riders to cross the entire continent in ten days flat. Each rider covered almost 120km (75 miles) a day, changing horses at the stations and fighting their way across deserts and through snowstorms before passing their mail satchel to a fresh horseman.

Thousands of miles of telegraph wire finally put the Pony Express out of business, but the image of the lone rider galloping through the wilderness had a lasting appeal for many people.

A tough, barrel-chested man named McCanles was the manager of the Rock Creek station. McCanles liked to throw his weight around, and was rough-handed with the men who worked for him, including the injured Wild Bill. Everyone at Rock Creek was relieved when McCanles sold his share of the business and moved away. But, in July 1861, the former manager returned with two friends and his son, complaining that the station's new owners owed him money. He tried to push his way past Wild Bill at the doorway to the ranch house, but Wild Bill threw him back. Moments later, McCanles and his friends were dead.

There is no reliable account of the Rock Creek gunfight. All we know for certain is that McCanles was shot at the entrance to the main cabin, while his friends were cut down in the station's dirt yard. His son escaped, running for his life in the confusion of the battle. Wild Bill was arrested and stood trial for the shootings, but he was released when the court decided he had only been trying to defend himself. McCanles was well known as a violent bully and most people assumed that the dead men had gone to the station looking for trouble.

The news of the gunfight spread quickly from town to town. It was whispered by firesides and shouted in saloons, and with each retelling it grew more and more fantastic – while the facts gradually blurred. This was how reputations were often made in the West, as a man's name became associated with a brutal killing or brave act. The story was quickly accepted into frontier folklore, and at its heart was an undeniable and startling truth. Three men had died at Rock Creek, and they died tackling Wild Bill Hickok.

While the Rock Creek story buzzed along the frontier, millions of soldiers were mustering for war in the north and south of the country. The United States had won independence from Britain in 1783, but by the middle of the 19th century the northern and southern states were growing apart. The curse of slavery was at the root of the problem.

Slavery had been a feature of American life for more than 200 years, but in 1860 the nation elected a bold anti-slavery president named Abraham Lincoln. Southern politicians feared that Lincoln would break the old alliances and understandings that had existed between the states that supported slavery and those that didn't. The Southerners had already lost the battle for Kansas and they resented pressure from the Northern states to change their local economies and traditions.

So, in February 1861, Southern politicians set up an independent government for a "Confederacy" of slave-owning states. Lincoln couldn't allow the Confederacy to break away from the American Union and, in April 1861, fighting broke out. The American Civil War, which lasted until 1865, was the bloodiest conflict in America's history.

The War changed the lives of millions of people. Fighting was particularly savage in Missouri, where local communities were made up of settlers from both North and South and attitudes towards slavery were often mixed. The young Jesse James (see page 58) was a product of these violent divisions in rural Missouri. He rode as a guerrilla fighter for the Confederate cause, ambushing and murdering northern supporters. But the North had its own secret troops and spies who operated outside military law – and Wild Bill was one of them.

When the fighting started, Wild Bill enlisted as a wagon driver and horseman for the Northern, or Union, forces. He was soon working as a scout and spy for the Union, providing information on enemy troop numbers and their movements across the Southern states. Often joining Confederate camps, posing as a new recruit, he marched along with the troops for several weeks before slipping away to make a report to his Northern officers. The Confederates were always on the lookout for spies, and Wild Bill had to be particularly careful when he was close to a battlefield. To many Union troopers, he was a familiar face, and couldn't risk being spotted by one of them. If a man called out a greeting, his true identity would be revealed and his cover would be blown.

There are dozens of stories about Wild Bill's wartime adventures – most of them beyond belief – but several writers have described his amazing swim across a river that separated the two battling armies. Wild Bill had been riding with a Confederate unit for weeks and was ready to steal away. But his unit was dug in by a wide river and guards were on patrol on every road and pathway around their camp. He didn't want to be shot as a deserter, but if he ran for the river both sides might start shooting at him: the Confederates would guess he was a spy and the Union troops on the opposite shore would think he was an enemy soldier.

When he overheard a sergeant boasting that he was the bravest man in the Confederate camp, Wild Bill saw his chance to escape. He challenged the sergeant to a dare, betting his horse that he would ride closer to the enemy – right to the shallows of the river. The sergeant accepted the bet and the two men raced out to cheers and whoops of encouragement from the Confederate troops.

Union sharpshooters spotted the riders and tried to knock them out of their saddles, but both men ducked down and rode grimly on. When they reached the river, a Union trooper on the opposite bank suddenly called out: "Don't shoot, boys, that's Wild Bill." The sergeant reached for his guns, but Wild Bill was quicker and shot him dead. As he plunged into the water, the furious Confederates realized they had been duped and opened fire. Bullets zipped all around him until he reached the safety of the Union shore.

The war gave Wild Bill his name and a reputation for bravery among Union army officers that would serve him well in the coming years. Following the North's victory in 1865, millions of men were demobilized from military units across America. In many states, they returned to burned-out homes, barren farms and ruined factories. It was a struggle for many of these ex-soldiers to earn a living, but Wild Bill could always find work as an army scout, tracking and rounding up stray animals, hunting deserters and guiding columns of cavalry across the prairies.

In 1867, he scouted for the maverick cavalry general, George Armstrong Custer (see page 42), who described Wild Bill as the type of man a novelist might gloat over. Custer had good reason to think of Wild Bill as an exaggerated fictional character. A journalist from the East, George Ward Nichols, had heard talk of the Hickok legend on a visit to the frontier in 1865. While Wild Bill rode onto the prairie with Custer, Nichols splashed his story across the newsstands of America.

Nichols first met Wild Bill in Springfield, Missouri, only weeks after a sensational murder trial had split the local community. Wild Bill had been gambling at cards when a man named Dave Tutt insulted him, accusing him of not paying his debts. Wild Bill admitted he owed Tutt some money and passed him a fistful of dollar bills. But Tutt wasn't satisfied.

Wanting to humiliate him in front of the other gamblers, he snatched Wild Bill's gold watch from the card table and dropped it into his own pocket. Wild Bill ordered Tutt to return the watch immediately, but Tutt just laughed and announced that he would wear the watch on a chain when he went walking around town at noon the next day.

"If you do, I'll shoot you dead," roared Wild Bill. But Tutt only chuckled and left the room.

Wild Bill and Tutt had crossed paths in the war, when there were whispers that Tutt was a spy for the Confederacy. More recently, the two men had argued over a local woman, and the people of Springfield had been expecting them to come to blows for several weeks. So nobody was surprised to see Wild Bill the following morning, waiting on the corner of the town's dirt square, checking his guns.

When Tutt appeared on the far side of the square, Wild Bill saw his watch glinting in the sun. The two men stepped towards each other and, when they were fifty paces apart, their hands flashed for their guns. A crackle of gunshots sounded simultaneously, deafening a crowd of bystanders who watched Tutt stagger and crash to the ground. Wild Bill had killed the man who had dared to mock him, shooting a bullet straight through his heart.

In all the battles, shootouts and showdowns in the history of the Western frontier, there were only a handful of gunfights where two men met on the street, walked slowly towards each other, then fired their guns. Fans of Western movies might think gunslingers always fought this way, but most battles were settled in far less even-sided contests. Men mostly waited in the dark for their rivals to go riding by and then shot them in the back. They ambushed them outside saloons, when they were drunk on whiskey, or while they dozed in the shuttered rooms of a boarding house. Survival in a gunfight usually came down to getting the advantage over your opponent.

But, when Wild Bill killed Dave Tutt, he set the pattern for the cinematic showdown between gunfighters – the insult, the threat, the long walk and the last draw. George Ward Nichols understood the power of this violent ritual to captivate his readers. He spent a week lounging in the Springfield saloons with Wild Bill, drinking in the scout's stories about McCanles, the Civil War and his other escapades.

When Nichols turned to his typewriter, he described Wild Bill in glowing terms, presenting all his exaggerated tales as proof of his daring, frontier spirit, incredible marksmanship and almost superhuman strength. *Harper's New Monthly* magazine published Nichols's article in February 1867. Wild Bill's newfound fame would hound him for the rest of his life.

Wild Bill played down many of the claims in Nichols's magazine story, but he quickly exploited public awareness of it to his advantage. He was still looking for a more permanent occupation, away from his army scouting missions and the long hours at the card table. When friends suggested that he try his hand at being a lawman in the bustling Kansas cow towns, Wild Bill used his reputation to win the support of local voters. In 1867, he was elected Sheriff of Hays, Kansas, and in 1871 he took up the post of Marshal in the mean streets of Abilene.

The cow towns were the last stop on the great cattle trails from Texas, where millions of animals were loaded onto railway cars and trundled back to the beef-hungry markets in the East. As the railway tracks probed deeper into the prairies, one cow town would fade and die while another sprung up around the new station. Saloons, gambling halls and stores appeared overnight, catering for the thirsty buffalo hunters, cowboys and soldiers who made their living there. It was the marshal's job to keep the peace, and safeguard the steady flow of dollar coins across the bars and gambling tables of the people who had elected him.

Some of the worst troublemakers were the cowboys – the men who guided the great herds of cattle across the plains to the railway stockyards. After months of dull, backbreaking work on the trail, cowboys stormed into the cow towns looking to drink the saloons dry and let off steam. Fights were common, and the men often rode back to camp in the morning with sore heads and empty pockets. A few cowboys were cold-hearted killers, on the run from the law in their home states. Wild Bill met the infamous gunslinger, John Wesley Hardin when, at the age of 18, he passed through Abilene, working as a cowboy.

In return for risking his life as a marshal, Wild Bill received a monthly salary of $150 and a share of certain fines and taxes. His reputation with a gun was enough to persuade most men to behave themselves, but he soon grew edgy and uncomfortable in the job. Wild Bill started walking in the middle of the street, avoiding the gloomy, plank walkways and alleyways around town, where attackers could hide. In Abilene, his nerves finally got the better of him. Wild Bill was caught in a gunfight in a dark street, and when he heard a noise behind him he whirled and fired his guns. He had shot and killed one of his own men, who had been running to help.

Wild Bill stayed on as Marshal of Abilene for several months after the shooting, but the accident must have persuaded him he wasn't cut out to be a lawman. He didn't enjoy the pressure of wearing a badge of authority and was tired of the constant bickering between cowboys and town residents. Wild Bill left Abilene early in 1872 and, after a year of scouting and gambling, he tried another change of career. This time, he joined his old friend, Buffalo Bill Cody, under the stage lights.

Cody was already a skilled theatrical entertainer by 1873 and had spotted the potential of a Western style show to pull in city audiences. He wanted Wild Bill to tell his stories on a national tour, beginning in New York. But, after his first night on stage, Wild Bill was longing to take the first train back to the frontier. He didn't want to let his friend down, but appearing in the show made him feel self-conscious and awkward.

Wild Bill had always been a soft-spoken man, and his voice was barely audible in the cavernous music halls. He squirmed uncomfortably under the heat and glare of the lights. Although, by all accounts, he was a gifted raconteur, he much preferred to entertain small groups of friends around a bar – rather than crowds of faceless strangers.

He also hated the necessary pretence involved in acting and using theatrical props. In one scene in the show, Wild Bill and Cody were supposed to be sharing a bottle of whiskey and telling yarns around the table in a frontier cabin. Each man would swig from the bottle and begin a story, but when Wild Bill took a drink he coughed and spat the liquid onto the floor. "That's cold tea," he complained, "and you don't get a story until I get real whiskey."

He was soon on his way home to the plains.

Wild Bill was in his late thirties when he abandoned the stage. He had tried most of the professions open to a man skilled with a gun on the frontier, but he couldn't stick with any of them. As he approached middle age, he wanted financial security and a more settled life. There was another pressing reason for him to retire. Wild Bill was having problems with his eyes.

After the Abilene shooting, people had wondered if the marshal's eyesight was failing. Wild Bill complained that his eyes were sore and sensitive to bright lights, and had even shot out a spotlight that was bothering him during his time in the music halls. He may have been suffering from pink eye – an irritating eye infection. In the days before antibiotics, pink eye could cause lasting damage to a person's vision. For a man who depended on his speed and accuracy with a gun, poor eyesight could be a death sentence.

In 1876, Wild Bill married a woman he had been courting in Cheyenne, Wyoming. Only a few months after the wedding, he gambled everything on a last effort to make his fortune and settle down. Wild Bill went hunting for gold.

In 1874, whispered stories of hunters stumbling across gold nuggets in the Black Hills of South Dakota had led the United States government to order a military survey of the area. General Custer commanded the expedition and found rich deposits of the precious metal. His discovery brought tens of thousands of prospectors tramping into the area, even though it was sacred ground to the local Sioux tribes and protected by a treaty. As the gold hunters trespassed into their land, the Sioux prepared for war, with fatal results for Custer and hundreds of his men, only two years later.

Some of the richest gold strikes were at a place known as Deadwood Gulch, where a town quickly grew up around the miners and their diggings. Wild Bill came to Deadwood in July 1876, hoping to stake his own gold claim and return to his new wife a richer man. But, just days after he arrived, he was struck by a sense of foreboding. He told a close friend that he didn't expect to leave the town alive.

Deadwood was a lawless, chaotic place – beyond the jurisdiction of the government. Rival saloon owners struggled for control of the town, as drifters, gamblers and gunfighters from across the West flocked there looking for easy money. Martha Jane Cannary – better known as 'Calamity Jane' – arrived in the same week as Wild Bill. She later claimed that Wild Bill loved her and that the pair had been married in a secret ceremony on the prairie.

Some writers have portrayed Calamity Jane as a buckskin-wearing frontier scout who could shoot faster, ride harder and drink more than most men in the West. But this sounds like a mirror image of Wild Bill and doesn't match the descriptions given by the people who knew her. She had no particular skill with a gun or horse and never rode as an army scout.

But there are strands of truth in every legend, and Calamity Jane *did* dress as a man, drink whiskey and wander the frontier in the footsteps of Custer, and then Wild Bill. She never married her buckskin hero, but perhaps she hoped to win him over during his stay in Deadwood? Instead, Calamity Jane was soon helping to bury the man she loved.

Instead of digging and exploring the land around town like a prospector, Wild Bill spent all his time at the card tables. He gambled more than ever, borrowing money from his friends and losing more gold than he won. The saloon owners who ran Deadwood began to suspect that Wild Bill was in town looking for a job as a lawman. But they were mistaken. In a tender letter he wrote to his wife on August 2, Wild Bill hinted that he expected to die very soon.

The following afternoon, Wild Bill left his room to find a game of poker. When he played cards, Wild Bill always liked to sit with his back to a wall and his eyes facing the saloon doors. But, on that day, his usual place was occupied and the other player refused to budge. Wild Bill shrugged and took a seat with his back to the bar. He didn't notice a nervous man push through the saloon doors and start edging his way along the bar. This man, whose name was Jack McCall, watched the players silently for a few minutes and then rushed forward, screaming, "Take that!" as he shot Wild Bill in the back of the head. Wild Bill's cards fluttered to the floor and he was dead.

McCall was caught and tried in Deadwood. He was found innocent – although he'd clearly done the deed – and there were whispers around town that the powerful saloon owners had bribed him to kill Wild Bill and then fixed his trial to set him free. McCall said he had shot Wild Bill to avenge the killing of his brother, but this proved to be a lie. When McCall left Deadwood, he was arrested and stood trial again, this time in a legitimate court. The jury found him guilty of murder and he was executed by hanging in 1877.

Prince of the Pistoleers

Wild Bill Hickok was buried in Deadwood, a small town in the wilderness like his birthplace, in a simple pine coffin. He is still remembered and celebrated today as one of the original pioneers – a true adventurer of the Wild West.

LAST STAND AT LITTLE BIG HORN

"The only good Indians I ever saw were dead."

General Philip Sheridan, commander of US army forces across the lands known as Indian Territory, hearing a Comanche chief call himself a good Indian.

George Armstrong Custer stopped his men high on a ridge overlooking the valley. Peering through powerful

binoculars, he could see thousands of lodges – or teepees – strung out for miles along the twisting riverbanks below. It was a breathtaking sight – the largest gathering of Native Americans for years – and Custer had made up his mind to destroy it. He glanced back at his men of the 7th Cavalry Regiment. They were exhausted after a month of hard riding on the hunt for this village. Many of them were raw recruits, still unsteady in the saddle and barely able to sight their rifles. His own Crow tribe scouts – sworn enemies of the people in the village – had warned Custer that he was dangerously outnumbered. Although they had offered to fight alongside him in any battle, they expected to die if he made an attack.

Custer knew that there were other US army units approaching the valley and he would only have to wait a day or two for them arrive. But he was not a man used to waiting. Staring down at the village, he could see women and children pulling down the hides, blankets and poles that held up their lodges. It looked as though they had spotted his soldiers and were trying to break down their homes and run. If he could smash the village with his force of just a few hundred riders, his name would be famous forever – from the raw frontier to the President's office in Washington.

He grinned and shouted: "Boys, we've got them." A moment later he ordered his bugler to sound the charge.

To build a new empire, a nation needs land. European settlers looking for a new life in America carved their empire out of the woods and prairies, in a war of conquest against the native people they found there. Some of the fiercest fighting in the Indian Wars, as they became known, took place in the Wild West.

It was the explorer, Columbus, who first used the word "Indian" to describe the original inhabitants of the Americas. In 1492, he set out on a mission to chart a new shipping route to Asia and ended up landing on an island in the Caribbean Sea. Thinking he must have arrived in India, Columbus greeted the local people as Indians. Although they quickly realized his mistake, other Europeans continued to use the term to describe the native people they encountered in this "New World" which eventually became known as America.

There were millions of Native Americans scattered across the continent in those days, living in thousands of small groups, known as tribes. By the 1800s their numbers had been reduced to around 300,000. Most of them died from epidemics of the infectious diseases imported by European colonists: smallpox, cholera, measles and influenza. Others were massacred as the settlers moved west, occupying their lands. Although some tribes fought back and were guilty of atrocities, they were no match for the power of the US government's soldiers and guns.

Most of the settlers in America thought they had every right to colonize the country, despite the sufferings of the tribes. In the 1840s, newspaper journalists, writers and politicians began talking of America's Manifest Destiny – the belief that the nation's development was inevitable and that the whole country would soon be dotted with farms, towns and sparkling cities. Some journalists described the tribes as murderous savages, or vermin. They saw them as a dangerous inconvenience in their quest to *civilize* the continent, and called for them to be wiped out like pests.

But America was vast, and in the early part of the 19th century, the United States government decided there was no need to destroy the Indians. Instead, they would exile them to the wilderness. In the 1830s the government set aside all the land "west of the Mississippi River" as permanent Indian Territory and promised that the tribes could live there, alone and in peace. They even ordered the army to construct a line of forts along the border of the territory, to keep the tribes in – and the settlers out.

Whether it was Manifest Destiny or simple human greed, it's hard to know, but miners, soldiers and settlers were soon tramping across Indian Territory in breach of their government's promises. The popular Oregon Trail snaked through the tribes' best hunting grounds and in 1846 American soldiers tramped through their sacred valleys and prairies, as they marched off to a war with Mexico.

After winning this war, the American government took possession of California and Texas. Then, after forest workers discovered gold in the California hills in 1848, the fragile peace was no longer sustainable.

Wagons rolled across the protected territory, as tens of thousands of prospectors rushed to the goldfields. They killed the game on the grass plains, cut down trees for firewood and polluted the rivers. Traders and towns followed after them, and the Native Americans saw their lands being invaded yet again.

Threatened with extinction, the tribes started butchering settlers, raiding villages and fighting soldiers across the Wild West. Each time there was an Indian war, there were massacres on both sides before peace could be restored with treaties and new promises from the government.

American politicians wanted the tribes to live in reservations – large camps where they were watched, fed and taught how to farm the land. In one sense, Indian Territory was the first reservation – a huge detention camp, fenced-in by army forts. But many settlers and politicians thought the government had been too generous and they demanded land from Indian Territory to make new states in the American Union. Eventually, bowing to pressure from land-hungry settlers, the government ordered the Native Americans to live on smaller reservations in the deserts or on barren mountainsides.

In 1868, tribal chiefs agreed to surrender most of Indian Territory in return for a fresh set of promises. They signed a treaty at Fort Laramie giving them permanent rights to the Black Hills in the Dakota region – a place with great religious significance for several tribes, including one of the most powerful in

America: the Sioux. When Custer's soldiers discovered gold in the Black Hills, the Sioux knew the whites would break their promises again. They left their reservations and gathered their allies to prepare for war.

The struggle for the Black Hills brought together three of the Wild West's most striking characters: Sitting Bull, Crazy Horse and General Custer.

Custer was a veteran of the Civil War and had been nicknamed "The Boy General" after becoming the Union army's youngest general at the age of 23. The rank was temporary and so he was only Lieutenant Colonel when he rode into battle with the Sioux. But many people still addressed him as General. He was a fearless rider, hunter and soldier, famed for his curly blond hair, fine uniforms and scarlet necktie. A flamboyant figure, he loved all the ceremonies of war. Custer had designed his own flag emblazoned with a pair of crossed swords. He took a pack of staghounds with him on the march and liked to charge at the enemy while a band of mounted musicians played an Irish drinking song, *Garryowen*.

Despite his bravery and good luck on the battlefields of the Civil War, he had a reputation for being reckless and impatient – at times risking the lives of his men in daring charges against the enemy lines. A story from his school days gives us a clue to Custer's true character. He was sitting by a closed window when a boy outside his classroom stopped and made a rude face at him. Without hesitating, Custer aimed a punch at his tormentor, smashing his fist through the glass. He was, in every sense, a man of action.

In May 1876, Custer and a large force of US troops left Fort Abraham Lincoln and made their way towards the Black Hills. Army generals knew that the Sioux were camping somewhere along the valley of Little Bighorn, close to the state border between Wyoming and Montana. Their orders were to crush any rebellion and return the warriors to their reservations. But they faced a dangerous opponent – an aggressive tribal chief who had refused to sign the Treaty of Laramie. His name was Sitting Bull.

Sitting Bull took his name from the bull buffalo, an animal that Native Americans believed to be both wise and strong. When he was still in his teens, Sitting Bull became a warrior, raiding deep into the lands of the nearby Crow tribe. He thought it was impossible for Native Americans to live alongside white settlers and had always urged his followers to shun confinement in reservations and to roam free on the plains.

When Sioux warriors learned that the army was marching towards their camp, they came to Sitting Bull for advice. Just weeks before Custer arrived at the valley, Sitting Bull took part in a religious ceremony known as the Sun Dance, hoping to experience a vision that would give him a glimpse into the future.

The Sun Dance was meant to be a brutal test of a warrior's strength and courage. In the same way that Custer had scorned the risk of pain when he punched his fist through a glass window, Sitting Bull would deliberately inflict pain on himself, as he attempted to enter a spirit world full of ghosts and visions. He began the ceremony by painting himself yellow like the Sun. Next, a warrior gouged one hundred pieces of flesh from Sitting Bull's extended arms, as an offering of the chief's body to his maker.

With the blood streaming from his arms, Sitting Bull began to circle around a tall pole in a shuffling dance. He danced like this for many hours with his face turned up to the Sun, until exhaustion and loss of blood made him pass out and collapse to the ground. As warriors splashed water in his face to revive him, Sitting Bull described the vision he had seen.

Soldiers and horses were falling from the sky, like a swarm of locusts rushing from a prairie fire. They dropped into the tribal village and Sioux warriors killed every one of them. When the slaughter was over, the warriors stepped carefully among the dead. They took no scalps – a clump of hair and skin cut from the crown of the head – or other booty from the enemy. Sitting Bull told his warriors that they would win the battle ahead, but they must be careful to respect his vision and leave the dead untouched. If the tribe ignored his warning, they risked being wiped from the face of the Earth.

Sitting Bull was not the only chief who believed in the power of visions. One of the Sioux nation's greatest warriors, Crazy Horse, had seen an image of an indestructible warrior in a dream when he was still a boy. He spent the rest of his life trying to turn himself into this phantom fighter.

Crazy Horse had been known as Curly before he became a warrior and took his father's name. He saw his vision after wandering deep into the mountains and going without food and water for three whole days. To keep himself awake, Curly lay down on a bed of sharp rocks and squeezed pebbles between his toes.

When he finally slipped into a trance, he saw his pony galloping towards him through shadows. The horse carried a brave warrior, naked apart from some strange markings on his body. White spots, like hail, were dotted over his skin and a streak of lightning ran down his face. The warrior carried no scalps or trophies taken from the enemies he had killed. Bullets and arrows couldn't hurt him and he rode safely through a violent storm.

Young boys in a tribe had to prove their bravery before they could become warriors, usually by killing a large animal – a wolf or bear – or joining a raid on an enemy tribe. When Curly was eighteen, he fought with some Arapahoe warriors. He killed two men and took their scalps, before an Arapaho hit him in the leg with an arrow. After the battle, Curly's father told him he was ready to be a warrior and gave him his name – Crazy Horse – as a reward for his courage. He also reminded his son of the vision and said the Arapaho arrow had struck him because he'd defied the dream warrior and scalped the enemy.

From then on, young Crazy Horse took no more scalps. He painted himself with white hail spots and a red lightning streak before riding off to war and threw a handful of dust into the air to symbolize the storm from his dream. Like his phantom warrior, he rode naked except for his moccasins and a strip of cloth tied around his waist. This was how Crazy Horse appeared to the US soldiers as they attacked the village at Little Bighorn – a screaming, wild-eyed figure, like something from a fevered dream.

On the morning of June 25, 1876, Custer's scouts climbed a hill and spotted a large herd of ponies and the blurry shape of lodges, several miles to the north. Custer had located the village a full day before he was scheduled to meet two large forces of US troops who were also approaching the river valley. He informed his officers that he would attack without delay, brushing aside the warnings from his scouts about the strength of the village.

Custer had no maps of the area, so he couldn't be sure of the best route for his raid. To cast a net around the village, he divided his regiment of almost 700 soldiers into four groups. He sent one unit to scout the country to the east and block any escape from the river valley, and left another to guard his pack animals. He ordered Major Reno and a force of around 140 men to advance up the Little Bighorn river. If they sighted the village, they were to attack at once. Custer rode off with the remaining 225 soldiers, following a ridge of hills that ran parallel to the river.

The Boy General had graduated last in his class at the West Point Military Academy but he knew enough about strategy to understand the power of a two-sided attack. If his men rushed around to the top end of the village, he could storm into the lodges at roughly the same time as Reno charged, catching the warriors in the jaws of a trap.

It was early in the afternoon when Major Reno took his men down to the river and made the crossing. He ordered a charge as soon as he spotted the edge of the village, a few hundred yards away. For a minute or two, he might have thought that Custer's brash confidence had been justified. Reno could see hundreds of lodges ahead of him, but no warriors. The only people who were out on the riverbanks or strolling between the lodges were women and children. They looked up in surprise at the charging soldiers and screamed as bullets ripped into their homes.

But, as the cavalry force turned a corner in the meandering river, Reno's men saw something that must have made their blood run cold. The village was much, much larger than they had expected. It stretched away for miles. Thousands of men were emerging from this sea of lodges, picking up weapons and mounting their horses. The warriors of the village had only been sleeping when Reno attacked. Most had gone to their beds at dawn, after spending the night celebrating a recent victory.

Realizing that he and his men would be butchered if they entered the village, Reno called off the charge. His soldiers climbed down from their horses and tried to form a defensive line, but Sioux warriors were soon picking them off with rifle shots. Reno was forced to retreat to a small island of trees. He tried to defend this island – hoping that Custer and his reinforcements would arrive at any second – but with his men dropping all around him he ordered a run for the hills. The water turned red as Crazy Horse and his warriors cut down the retreating soldiers. Reno and most of his unit just made it to the top of a grassy hill and dug in to prepare for a siege.

While Reno and his men were fighting for their lives, Custer was galloping across the hills to the north. His soldiers – and their horses – were exhausted, but they still hadn't reached the top of the village. Custer finally turned his men and came down to the river at a point opposite the middle of the tented city. He might have been hoping to charge across and attack the heart of the camp, before turning to the south and joining Reno's force.

But Custer never crossed the river. As he stared at the wall of white lodges on the far bank, the Boy General must have known he was in trouble. Groups of warriors were already racing towards him, "like bees swarming out of a hive," as one Blackfoot chief later described it. Custer ordered a retreat. His soldiers spurred their horses on up the narrow ravines and wooded clefts in the hills, in an attempt to return to the high ground. But more than a thousand Sioux warriors pursued them, knocking soldiers out of their saddles with hatchets and clubs and sending arrows hissing though the air.

In close fighting, the Native Americans' bow and arrow was a fearful weapon. While handguns had little effect on the tough hide of a buffalo, an arrow could kill a charging bull. One soldier claimed that he had seen warriors shoot their arrows though inch-thick wooden planks. Another said that a strong warrior could send an arrow right through a full-grown buffalo, pick the arrow up from the prairie floor and shoot it again.

The Native Americans carved their arrowheads from razor-sharp triangles of flint, which inflicted deep, crippling wounds. Warriors usually carried a fistful of arrows into battle and could shoot several into the air before the first had struck its target. Many of the dead soldiers at Little Bighorn were found bristling with dozens of arrow shafts.

Custer led his men out of the ravines and onto the hills. If they could reach the high ground, the soldiers would have a better chance of digging in and keeping the warriors at bay with their rifles. But, as Custer and his men climbed the slope, they saw hundreds of warriors on horses riding over the summit. Custer and his men were surrounded.

The advancing warriors must have been a terrifying sight for the inexperienced troops. Sioux fighters screamed and whooped as they circled the soldiers. Their bodies were painted in bright, flashing reds, sky blues and bands of black stripes. Many wore animal skins, bear claws, eagle feathers and buffalo horns. They rushed in among the frightened soldiers, hacking and tearing at their bodies in close combat. Ignoring Sitting Bull's warning, they scalped the dead where they fell.

Under the endless Montana skies, Custer and his entire force of more than 220 men were destroyed. The other units of the regiment gathered around Major Reno's hilltop camp. They were under attack until the following morning, when the rest of the US army troops from Fort Abraham Lincoln arrived in the valley and the Sioux broke down their village and fled.

Custer's Last Stand, as it quickly became known, outraged people across America and hardened public attitudes to the rights of the native tribes. Newspapers carried lurid descriptions of the dead soldiers. Most had been scalped and their bodies mutilated so badly they were impossible to recognize. These atrocities persuaded many Americans who had once been sympathetic to the tribes that they were no better than wild animals. As Sitting Bull had predicted, the army hounded his people out of the country, chasing them into Canada where they began to starve.

Custer's actions in the battle still spark arguments today. Some people call him a military hero, while others brand him a reckless fool. Reckless or not, his Last Stand was the final large-scale battle between the army and the tribes. The government strengthened its military forces across the West, and most Native Americans were forced to resign themselves to life on a reservation.

The last moments of Custer and his men, trapped on a grassy hill inside a spinning wheel of howling warriors, has become one of the Wild West's most famous images. And the disputes over the eerie Black Hills have never ended. In the 1980s, lawyers acting for the Sioux nation won compensation from the US government for the illegal occupation of their lands more than 100 years earlier.

THE PRIVATE WAR OF JESSE JAMES

"We are the boys that are hard to handle and will make it hot for the party that ever tries to take us."

Jesse James, in a letter to a Kansas newspaper, 1879

The conductor on board the no. 7 train leaned out and saw the shape of a man in the distance, waving a red flag.

"What's all this?" blurted the conductor, as his train slowed to a halt. The no. 7 wasn't scheduled to stop at the village of Gads Hill in this remote corner of Missouri, but the red flag was a warning signal for trouble on the line and the train driver couldn't ignore it. As the conductor dropped to the ground, a man rushed towards him through the clouds of smoke and steam from the engine.

"If you move, you die," snapped the man, lifting the muzzle of a revolver to the conductor's face.

The conductor looked up at the outlaw and shuddered. He was wearing a white "spook mask" over his head – a cotton sack with rough-cut holes for his eyes and nose. There were four other men on the platform behind him, all wearing the same ghostly headgear.

"We aim to rob this train and everyone aboard it," shouted one of the men. "So you passengers keep your heads inside and don't move."

The robbers went about their work like a squad of well-trained soldiers. One man stayed with the conductor on the platform, guarding a small group of villagers. Two others boarded the train and made their way towards the baggage car, while the last two walked along the tracks on either side of the train, pointing their shotguns up at the windows. When the outlaws barged into the baggage car they discovered the express company messenger trembling with fear. In the days before a reliable and secure mail system, "express companies" delivered documents, cash and other valuables for their clients. They employed messengers to watch over their shipments, but these men were clerks or accountants – not gunslingers. The messenger handed his keys to the outlaws and they quickly ransacked the safe.

"Let's take a walk," growled one of the bandits, when he'd emptied every letter and package.

The two men strolled through the train cars, waving their revolvers and snatching money and valuables from the terrified passengers. They kept up a lively banter with their victims and even swapped hats with one man. With over $2000 stuffed in their pockets, they jumped down to the platform and waved to the rest of the gang to join them with the horses.

"Get this to a newspaper," joked the leader of the outlaws and he dropped a piece of paper to the ground. The stunned conductor watched the bandits ride away *before he picked up their note. It described a daring raid on the no. 7 train. The outlaws had written their own press release, hours before the robbery, and followed the story to the letter.*

The train hold-up at Gads Hill in January 1874 was typical of the string of robberies committed by Jesse James and his notorious gang of thieves. They were a disciplined bunch, greedy, armed to the teeth and always calm under pressure. But the startling boldness of the newspaper note left at Gads Hill tells us more about Jesse's character than his cool-headed, military approach to crime.

Jesse James craved publicity. For much of his outlaw life, he presented himself as a wronged man – an avenger for the white citizens of the southern American states who, he claimed, had been persecuted and abused since their defeat in the four-year Civil War. Jesse's supporters even tried to portray him as an American Robin Hood, robbing the bullying corporations, bankers and train companies of the North and helping the destitute farmers and settlers of the South. But, according to most accounts, Jesse never gave a dime to the poor or the needy. He was a bitter old soldier and outcast, striking back at the forces of change in his homeland and refusing to accept that the Civil War was over.

Jesse Woodson James was born on September 5, 1847, in Clay County, western Missouri. His father, Robert James, was a Baptist preacher who left his rural parish to join the California Gold Rush in 1849. Robert died of cholera before he found any gold, leaving Jesse's mother, Zerelda, to raise a young family and run a small farm. Zerelda was a strong and forthright woman who ruled the roost when she remarried – to the timid Dr. Samuel. She had been born in Kentucky and raised her sons to respect the customs and traditions of America's southern states – including the right to own slaves.

Jesse was still a boy when fighting broke out in Kansas, just a few miles from Clay County, to decide whether the new territory should be a free state or a slave-owning one. Friends of the James family rode into Kansas to battle for the pro-slavery movement and the vicious dispute was still simmering when   the

Confederacy of Southern states broke away from the American Union over the same issue.

Jesse's elder brother, Frank, enlisted in the Confederate army when the fighting started in 1861, but Jesse was too young to join him. But the war rumbled on and, three years later, the boy with the slim build, piercing blue eyes and sandy hair was riding with one of the most bloodthirsty gangs of guerrilla soldiers in Missouri, risking his life for the South.

Jesse James was only 17 when he volunteered to ride with William 'Bloody Bill' Anderson and his bushwhackers – a band of roaming killers who fought for the same cause as the Southern army, but who wore no uniform and ignored military laws. The war was going badly for the Confederates, as most of Missouri was under Union control. This border state was sandwiched between the two and the fighting was particularly savage.

Friends and families with different views on slavery turned on each other, burning homes and crops in a frenzy of hate. Jesse had witnessed his stepfather being tortured by a Union mob in 1863 and he wanted bloody revenge on the soldiers of the North. In September 1864, he took part in one of the worst atrocities of the War, when Anderson's gang raided the small town of Centralia, Missouri.

Around 80 bushwhackers stormed into the town, kicking down doors, dragging families into the streets and stealing anything they could carry from their houses. When a train approached the Centralia station Anderson's men fired at the engineer and driver, forcing them to stop. The bushwhackers climbed aboard to rob the passengers and discovered 23 Union soldiers sitting quietly in one of the cars. These men were returning home on leave from the battlefields and were carrying no weapons.

Anderson ordered the soldiers off the train and told them to line up on the platform. He shot two men who hesitated on the train steps, took a sergeant hostage – and then commanded his guerrillas to execute the rest. Gun smoke billowed across the platform as the bushwhackers emptied their revolvers into the ranks of unarmed men. They scalped two of the corpses, set fire to the train and rode out of town.

As news of the massacre spread, a detachment of over 100 Union soldiers chased the bushwhackers into the Missouri woods. Commanded by Major Andrew Johnston, the troopers were raw recruits with no combat experience. They stood little chance against Anderson's cut-throats. The bushwhackers lured them into a trap, charged their lines and shot them down.

Jesse rode at the front of the charge, shouting a war cry and firing a pair of revolvers. It was he who killed the major with a shot through the head. When the shooting was over, the guerrillas robbed and mutilated the dead. It was this kind of carnage, horror and destruction that characterized the career of the outlaw Jesse James.

Jesse was not the only person to be scarred and changed by the savagery of the Civil War. When the South surrendered in 1865, millions of people had been sucked into the conflict, losing their homes, their loved ones and even their way of life. Most Confederate supporters tried to adjust to the changes across the South and the new power of northern politicians, but Zerelda and her boys just couldn't put the past behind them. They resented the officials, businessmen and bankers who had supported the North during the war and now prospered across Missouri. Like many former bushwhackers, Jesse and Frank still wanted to punish their northern enemies.

On February 13, 1866, two men in long soldiers' coats stepped into the Clay County Savings Bank in Liberty, Missouri and asked the cashier to change a $10 bill. When the cashier got to his feet to get the money, the two men drew their revolvers and announced that they were robbing his bank. The cashier must have been startled by their words. This was the first daylight bank robbery by outlaws in American history.

The cashier handed over almost $60,000 in gold and cash and the outlaws shut him in the bank's vault. But they forgot to lock the vault door and the cashier rushed to a window to see at least a dozen riders out in the street, shooting their revolvers into the air and screaming as they charged through the town. One of the gang shot and killed a teenage boy, before galloping out of Liberty and disappearing into the woods. This senseless murder and the gang's display of firepower in the street reminded people of the brutal tactics used by the bushwhackers. Now the War was over, Jesse and Frank had turned into hardened criminals.

The raid on Liberty marked the beginning of a fourteen-year career as an outlaw for Jesse James. He robbed banks, trains and stagecoaches across the West, recruiting veterans of the War into his gang and using their combat skills to keep one step ahead of the law. With no organized national police force to track him down, Jesse easily avoided the small town sheriffs and posses that came after his gang.

But he had another huge advantage over the police. Local people knew he was a killer and a bandit but many of them were still sympathetic to the Confederate cause. They helped Jesse to hide from lawmen and gave him fresh horses, food and shelter whenever he needed it. Not everyone in Clay County was a friend of Jesse James, but he had a network of supporters who had promised never to betray him.

After years of losing precious shipments to the gang, a group of Express companies hired a gruff Scotsman named Allan Pinkerton to capture Jesse. The Pinkerton Detective Agency used the motto, "We Never Sleep," in their newspaper advertisements. Company agents were renowned for working undercover on dangerous assignments. In March 1874, Allan Pinkerton sent one of his best men to infiltrate the James gang.

Joseph Whicher arrived in Clay County and immediately presented himself as a Pinkerton agent to the sheriff in Liberty.

"What are you planning to do out here?" asked the amazed sheriff.

Whicher explained that he was going to visit Zerelda James's house and ask for work as a farm hand. Once he'd won the trust of the family, he would produce a gun and deliver Frank and Jesse to the sheriff.

"You'll never find the James boys," cried the sheriff. "They live out in the woods or in lonely farmhouses with their friends. If you do find them, they'll kill you. And if they don't kill you, the old woman will."

The Pinkerton Agency was one of the most effective detective groups of the 19th century. It pioneered the use of the mug shot – an accurate photo or sketch of an individual – in a vast database of criminals and suspects which was stored at the company's Chicago headquarters. But, despite all their successes fighting crime in America's cities, Pinkerton agents didn't quite understand the importance of the close ties between families and friends that existed in rural Missouri. Whicher ignored the sheriff's warning and his body was discovered the following day, shot three times.

Allan Pinkerton immediately dispatched two agents to investigate Whicher's murder. But they too were murdered within a few days of arriving in western Missouri. The loss of three agents enraged Pinkerton and he sent a raiding party to attack the James's farm and arrest Jesse and Frank. In January the following year, Pinkerton agents surrounded the house and hurled a smoke bomb through a window – to drive the James boys out of the building.

But Frank and Jesse were in another part of the country that night. The device landed in a fire and exploded, killing Jesse's young half-brother and wounding Zerelda. Shocked by the screams coming from the house, the Pinkertons fled into the woods.

The raid was a disaster for Allan Pinkerton. Jesse and Frank had evaded him, his agents had murdered a child, and people across Missouri were asking if the James brothers were being unfairly persecuted for their actions during the War. Jesse wrote several letters to newspaper editors claiming that he was an innocent man. He explained that he was too scared to give himself up to the law in Missouri, in case a northern mob – or detective agency – lynched him before he could stand trial.

While he was penning these notes, Jesse continued to rob banks and trains. His growing fame must have swelled his confidence and criminal ambitions. In September 1876, he took his gang hundreds of miles away from their usual territory to attack a small town in Minnesota.

Jesse James came to Northfield to rob the First National Bank and to humble his enemies in the North. There was nothing particularly notable or unusual about Northfield, but it was home to a man who had fought bravely for the Union and earned the lasting contempt of old Confederate fighters. General Adelbert Ames was a gifted soldier who had been appointed as Governor of Mississippi after the war. After being hounded out of office by Southern politicians, Ames had retired to Northfield to help run a mill with his father. The Ames fortune was invested in the First National Bank.

Jesse James rode into town with seven other riders: his brother Frank, the three Younger brothers, Charlie Pitts, Clell Miller and Bill Chadwell. Only two of the gang would survive the raid and the following manhunt.

While the rest of the outlaws took up positions around the town, Pitts and the James boys stepped into the bank and drew their guns. An ex-Union soldier named Heywood was the cashier that day. He stood up to face the outlaws, told them that the safe was locked and flatly refused to open it.

One of the raiders pressed a knife against Heywood's throat, but the plucky cashier broke free and shouted for help. The raider knocked him to the floor with the butt of his revolver. When Heywood still refused to touch the safe, one of the outlaws fired his revolver only inches from his head.

In the seconds after the shot, Jesse called for silence, to listen for any sounds of alarm from the town. He was dismayed when he heard the snap of a rifle shot, followed by the roar of several guns blasting outside. Jesse peered through a window and saw Cole Younger and the rest of his gang shooting from their horses. The residents of Northfield had guessed what was happening and had armed themselves with shotguns and Winchester rifles.

Miller was the first of the gang to go down, blasted from his horse by a shotgun blast. Cole Younger took a bullet in the hip as he went to help Miller. He clambered back onto his horse just as Bill Chadwell was shot and killed by a man named Manning, the owner of the Northfield hardware store. Adelbert Ames had walked over from his mill and was standing next to Manning when he shot Chadwell. As Bob Younger started to return fire at Manning and Ames, he was hit in the arm and had to drop his gun. Cole saw the blood spurting from his brother's arm and kicked his horse towards the bank doors. He leaned down and shouted to Jesse: "They're killing us out here." It was time to go.

The three bandits darted out of the bank empty-handed, but not before one of them raised a pistol and shot Heywood dead. The brave cashier had defied Jesse James and he paid for it with his life. And the door to the safe had stood unlocked throughout the attempted robbery.

Under fire, Jesse made it to his horse and rallied his gang, while cursing his luck. But Jim Younger's shoulder exploded under the impact of a bullet as they stormed out of town. The Youngers were badly wounded, Miller and Chadwell were dead in the street, and Jesse's plan to strike back at his old foe had ended in humiliating defeat.

But worse was to come, as a posse killed Pitts and trapped the Youngers within a few weeks. Ames visited Cole and questioned him about the robbery through the bars of his cell, shortly before the old bushwhacker was sentenced to life in prison.

Only Jesse and Frank escaped, crossing hundreds of miles of rough country on foot while a posse snapped at their heels. When the brothers finally reached Missouri they gathered up their families and set off to Nashville, Tennessee. Frank bought a ranch, put his guns away and started a new life as a farmer. Jesse set up home with his wife and young children, using the alias J. D. Howard. Bruised and bloodied after Northfield, the James brothers had decided to give up the outlaw trail.

The Private War of Jesse James

When soldiers return from battle they often find it hard to settle back into civilian life. Despite all its horrors, veterans who have served for years in a combat zone can grow addicted to the strange passions and daily shocks of war. While Frank James learned to love the routines of farming work, Jesse began to itch for his old life as a bandit. He was bored and restless in Nashville and he gambled his money away at cards and on horse races, looking for the same risks and thrills he had taken for granted as the leader of a gang. Jesse missed his notoriety and seeing his name in the papers. He missed his cause.

But the world around Jesse James had changed. By 1879, the southern states had managed to claw back much of their independence from the North. There was no slavery in the South, but black Americans suffered oppression under racist laws, attitudes and institutions. It would be years before they could claim the same rights as their white counterparts. Southern politicians had regained power across much of the region and many people were looking to the future and trying to forget the past.

When Jesse raised another gang – without Frank – he found that his old network of friends had moved with the times. Most of the old bushwhackers were dead, so he had to recruit strangers into his gang. The riders he picked were common thieves and thugs. They had been too young to fight in the war, so they lacked the discipline and training of soldiers. Jesse couldn't trust them.

After a spate of killings and desertions, he was left with just two men – brothers Bob and Charley Ford. But while Jesse planned new heists and attacks on trains, Bob Ford held a secret meeting with the Governor of Missouri. The governor offered Ford thousands of dollars in reward money and a full pardon for all his crimes – including the murder of Jesse James. Ford accepted the deal.

On April 3, 1882, Jesse was sitting chatting with the Ford brothers in the breakfast room of his new house in St. Joseph, Missouri. Bob Ford didn't want to risk a face-to-face gunfight with Jesse. He had been waiting for a chance to shoot his friend in the back. But Jesse never dressed without his guns and Ford was sure that the old outlaw suspected his treachery.

Jesse suddenly got up from the table and unbuckled his gun belt, saying he would be carrying boxes in and out of the yard that morning and anyone walking by might think it was strange that he was so heavily armed. He walked over to a picture frame hanging on the wall and complained that it was dusty. Turning his back on the Ford brothers, he stepped onto a chair by the wall and began to sweep the frame. Bob Ford shot him in the head at point-blank range.

It was an unexpected, sacrificial death for a man who had lived by the gun for so many years, as though Jesse realized that he had outlived his times. Dropping his guns and turning around he had quietly offered himself up to his assassin.

Despite all his terrible crimes, Jesse still had a few loyal fans who always believed he was a freedom fighter for Missouri. Only weeks after his death, a popular song portrayed him as an outlaw hero and he quickly became another legend of the Wild West.

Jesse James was a lad who killed many a man,
He robbed the Glendale train,
He stole from the rich and he gave to the poor
He'd a hand and a heart and a brain.
Poor Jesse had a wife to mourn for his life,
Three children, they were brave.
But that dirty little coward that shot Mr. Howard
Has laid poor Jesse in his grave.

A CHILD OF THE WEST

"I wasn't the leader of any gang. I was for Billy all the time."

Billy the Kid, to a reporter, after his capture by Sheriff Pat Garrett

There was no love lost between Billy the Kid and his guard at the Lincoln courthouse, Bob Olinger. They had fought on opposite sides during the recent gunfights around Lincoln County, New Mexico, and Olinger never lost a chance to bully and taunt The Kid in the days leading up to his execution.

"You won't dodge me or the hangman this time,"

laughed Olinger, as he loaded both barrels of his shotgun. The Kid only smiled and whispered: "Careful you don't shoot yourself, Bob."

Lincoln had no secure jail and Sheriff Pat Garrett was holding The Kid in a first-floor room of the courthouse. Garrett was out of town but he had left Olinger and his other deputy, James Bell, to watch over The Kid. He warned them not to underestimate the young killer and to keep him shackled at all times. The days passed slowly, with The Kid and Bell playing cards and telling stories while Olinger sat scowling in a corner.

Olinger was across the street having dinner one evening when Billy told Bell he needed to go to the bathroom. Bell liked The Kid, but he kept him shackled as they walked downstairs and into the yard. On their return, Billy started up the stairs ahead of Bell and turned to step into the hallway. The deputy lagged behind and didn't see Billy slip his slender wrists out of the handcuffs. As Bell entered the hall, Billy swung the heavy, iron hoops and knocked him to the floor. Bell lifted his hands to his broken face as The Kid reached down and snatched his revolver.

"Don't you run," he shouted, but Bell jumped to his feet and clattered down the stairs, making for the yard. Billy shot him in the back. Olinger heard the blast, dropped his knife and fork and came running. When he was halfway across the street, a cowboy shouted: "Bonney's killed Bell." The deputy stopped in his tracks. He looked up at the courtroom balcony and saw The Kid staring down at him. He was holding Olinger's shotgun and smiling.

A Child of the West

"Yeah," sighed Olinger, "and he's killed me too."
Billy gave him both barrels.

Billy the Kid is a Wild West mystery, a ghost rider and will-o'-the-wisp who still haunts the vast landscapes of New Mexico. When most people hear his name, they imagine a fresh-faced cowboy who was brave and heroic, fighting corrupt businessmen and cattle ranchers and risking his life for his friends. Everybody remembers that he was young, carefree and charming.

But Billy was a cold-blooded killer too – a teenage runaway on the Western frontier, dragged into a vicious battle for survival before he had a chance to grow up into a man. There were many sides and faces to this Western legend.

Henry McCarty was born in New York City in 1859, thousands of miles from the wild, desert country where he became famous as The Kid. He was the son of Irish emigrants who had sailed to the New World to escape famine and poverty at home. Poor and unskilled, his parents joined the throng of new arrivals trapped in the squalor and stench of New York's overcrowded slums. Walled in by factories, warehouses and teeming apartment blocks, the newcomers were quickly worn down by hard work and disease.

Henry's father died or drifted away and his mother moved to Silver City, New Mexico, drawn to the clean air and open spaces of the American frontier. She remarried in 1873, to a man named Antrim, but less than two years later she died of tuberculosis. Henry's stepfather was a decent man but he was away for months on end, prospecting in the hills. With no parent or guardian to watch over him, Henry teamed up with a hard-drinking rogue known as "Sombrero Jack" and soon ran into trouble with the law.

Henry's first crime was almost comical: raging with whiskey, Sombrero Jack persuaded him to hide some clothes he'd stolen from a Chinese laundry. Henry's landlady found the clothes in his room and informed the sheriff, who decided to lock Henry in his jail for a few hours to teach him a lesson. When the sheriff returned, he discovered that his slim-hipped, fifteen-year-old captive had shinned up the chimney and escaped. Henry's crime and prison breakout might seem ridiculous, but they hint at his resourcefulness and lack of respect for the law. They also set him on the path towards more serious crimes, as he ran from Silver City into the badlands of Arizona.

For the next two years Henry Antrim scraped a living as a ranch-hand and cattle rustler (or thief) in the country around Camp Grant, Arizona. He learned all the usual frontier skills and vices – how to ride, shoot and gamble with cards – but he rarely drank alcohol, perhaps as a result of the drunken fiasco at the Silver City laundry.

With his fresh-faced expression, ready smile and slim build, Henry's friends joked that he was too young and petite to be a cowboy and they nicknamed him The Kid. Everyone he met was struck by his charm and youthfulness and he made friends easily.

But a few men thought The Kid looked like an easy target to bully. They were making a big mistake. One of the blacksmiths at Camp Grant, Francis 'Windy' Cahill, picked on The Kid when he walked into a saloon, tripping him and mocking him in front of a crowd at the bar. The Kid didn't back down and, when Cahill threw a punch, The Kid shot him in the stomach. Cahill died the next day and Henry Antrim crossed back into New Mexico to avoid arrest and trial for his murder.

It was 1877 when The Kid arrived in Lincoln

County, New Mexico, riding with a gang of rustlers and gunslingers who called themselves The Boys. He was still only seventeen, but he was used to the company of outlaws and had already killed his first man. At some point in his travels, The Kid had learned to speak Spanish fluently and he seemed more at home with the poor Hispanic settlers than the rich, white farmers and merchants who lived around Lincoln. This time he went by a new name: William Bonney. The Boys called him Billy, but his old friends in New Mexico still knew him as The Kid. It was only a matter of time before people dubbed him Billy the Kid.

The Kid didn't stay with The Boys for long. Although he had rustled horses and shot a man while defending himself, Billy was no criminal thug or sadistic killer like the men in the gang. The Boys were hired guns who worked for James Dolan, one of the most powerful merchants in Lincoln. Dolan supplied beef to the army troops guarding nearby reservations and ran a store in the town. Known as The House, Dolan's store held a brutal monopoly on the supplies and equipment that local farmers needed to survive. Dolan was determined to protect his business empire and he used The Boys to intimidate and attack any competitors.

Billy was a tough fighter and survivor, but there was a softer side to his character. He loved music, books, singing and dancing, and he was soon finding pals among the hard-working ranchers and cowboys around Lincoln. He quit The Boys and took a job as a ranch hand for an Englishman named John Tunstall.

A cultured and exotic figure on the frontier, Tunstall was struggling to run a ranch, build a large herd of cattle and open his own store in town. Although he was never a close friend, Billy respected his employer and must have breathed a sigh of relief that he had broken away from men like The Boys. His new job was a chance to go straight and leave his wild years behind him, but any hopes he had for a better life were crushed when Dolan seized Tunstall's store and tried to put him out of business.

The Lincoln County War – as it became known – was no ordinary gunfight. Billy and the other cowboys who took Tunstall's side in the struggle fought for months like soldiers, using every tactic and trick they could think of to smash their opponents. Nobody was prepared to surrender or show any weakness. The Lincoln fighters all lived by a strict and aggressive code that demanded loyalty to your friends and contempt for your enemies. Both sides exploited the workings of the legal system to legitimize their actions. They bribed or persuaded weak officials to issue arrest warrants for petty crimes and deputized their gunmen to bring in the wanted men.

A Child of the West

In February 1878, Billy and Tunstall had a run-in with one of these posses – a gang of The Boys riding for Dolan, with orders to capture some livestock that Tunstall was herding across open desert towards his ranch. Billy spotted The Boys and spurred his horse up a hillside, taking shelter behind some rocks, but Tunstall turned to confront his pursuers. Three of the Boys shot him off his horse. They claimed later that the Englishman had resisted arrest, but few people believed it.

When Billy went to pay his respects to his murdered employer, he gave the corpse a blood-chilling promise: "Don't you worry. I'll get a few of them before I die."

Dick Brewer had been Tunstall's ranch foreman and he quickly organized the dead man's cowboys and friends into a fighting force. Calling themselves The Regulators, they each vowed to avenge Tunstall's murder. Brewer asked a local police constable to issue warrants for the arrest of The Boys and to deputize his men. The constable agreed, but Dolan was close friends with Lincoln's sheriff, William Brady, and he used his influence to challenge the legality of Brewer's warrants. Brady would pay a high price for siding with Dolan and his cowboy mercenaries.

Despite the uncertainty over their legal status, the Regulators formed a posse and in just a few weeks they had gunned down three of Dolan's gang. These tit-for-tat killings were only the start of the bloodletting across Lincoln County.

A Child of the West

On April 1, a group of Brewer's gunmen hid themselves behind a wall on the main street of Lincoln. When Sheriff Brady and four of Dolan's 'deputies' walked past, the assassins opened fire. Brady was hit a dozen times and died in the street. When the shooting stopped, Billy the Kid hurdled the wall and sprinted over to the sheriff's body. He was planning to rifle Brady's pockets for the arrest warrants made out against The Regulators, but one of The Boys was watching from a hotel window and he shot Billy through the thigh with his Winchester rifle.

Billy ran for cover, vaulting the wall to rejoin his friends. He wasn't seriously injured but he had shown his face to several witnesses along the street. For the rest of his short life the murder of Brady continued to haunt him, in a chain of bloody events that only ended with his death.

Three days after they had murdered Lincoln's sheriff, The Regulators caught up with another man from Dolan's gang. Andrew 'Buckshot' Roberts was a gritty veteran of the frontier, an old buffalo hunter and brawler who refused to surrender to Brewer and his men. In a chaotic shootout, Roberts wounded several Regulators and shot Brewer through the eye before dying of his own gunshot wounds. Shocked by the loss of Brewer, The Regulators rode into the mountains to hide from the Boys and plot their next move.

After two months of skirmishes and rising tensions across the County, they gathered at the Lincoln home of Tunstall's lawyer, Alexander McSween, for a final showdown with the Dolan gang. For five days the cowboys and their supporters traded shots, threats and insults, but when Dolan persuaded the local army commander to intervene with a squad of troops, the Regulators' friends panicked and ran. The Boys set fire to McSween's house, driving the last, diehard Regulators into the street. McSween was shot down as Billy ran for his life under the cover of darkness.

Now that Tunstall, his foreman and his lawyer were all dead, most people thought The Regulators had lost the war. Billy joined a group of his friends riding down to Texas to sell rustled horses and make plans for the future.

Some of the men were happy to put New Mexico behind them. But The Kid missed the tight-knit community of cowboys and settlers around Lincoln County who had befriended him. Tired of running away from his troubles, he decided to return to the state in December 1878, hiding out at a crumbling, isolated army camp named Fort Sumner.

The small crowd of farmers and cowboys living at the fort welcomed The Kid, and even offered to protect him from any posses they saw snooping in the area. Billy accepted their help, but he knew that he would soon be caught and tried for Sheriff Brady's murder unless he could clear his name with the local authorities. When the American President appointed a new governor for the state, Billy saw his chance to win a pardon and put the outlaw life behind him forever.

Governor Lewis Wallace arrived in Santa Fe, New Mexico, determined to restore law and order in Lincoln. He offered an amnesty to every man who had taken part in the fighting, as long as there were no outstanding warrants for his arrest. But the governor's offer excluded The Kid.

In March 1879, Billy sent a series of handwritten notes to Wallace outlining a secret proposal. He would testify against Dolan and The Boys, in return for a promise by Wallace that he wouldn't be tried for the murder of Brady. At an extraordinary, midnight meeting between the governor and the young outlaw, Wallace agreed to The Kid's request.

Billy gave himself up for arrest and kept his end of the deal in the witness box. But a few days into the case, the District Attorney revealed that he was determined to prosecute Billy and see him hang for killing Brady. The Kid tried to get a message to Wallace asking for him to stand by their arrangement, but the governor ignored his appeal. Wallace was a complex and rather aloof individual who was immersed in a lengthy book he was writing at the time: *Ben Hur*.

While Wallace scribbled away at his masterpiece, Billy did what he had always done when his life was suddenly put at risk – he slipped his chains and ran for the hills. Wallace's betrayal was a bitter blow to Billy. It left him with no other choice but to remain an outlaw. He rode back to Fort Sumner and recruited some friends from The Regulator days to join him rustling horses and cattle.

A Child of the West

Billy's evidence had helped to convict some of the ringleaders in the Lincoln County War, but it also made him a front-page news story. As his notoriety spread across the West, he became a source of embarrassment for the authorities and a burden for local people. Brady's friends were demanding The Kid's arrest and livestock owners protested about the brazen rustling of his gang. In November 1880, the citizens of Lincoln elected Sheriff Pat Garrett after he promised that he would bring The Kid in.

Garrett had been a cowboy and bartender at Fort Sumner in 1878 and he knew The Kid. He was a tall, powerful man who had hunted buffalo on the plains before arriving in New Mexico. A month after his election, Garrett and his posse tracked Billy and four of his men to a lonely spot known as Stinking Springs. The outlaws were asleep inside a goatherd's stone hut, so Garrett staked his deputies on every side of the building and told them to shoot to kill, the moment Billy stepped outside. At dawn, a man in a broad sombrero came out of the hut to feed the horses. Garrett mistook him for Billy and shot him dead with his Winchester.

Billy and the other men inside the hut tried to fight their way out, but Garrett and his deputies were armed with rifles and they covered every escape. In the late afternoon Billy surrendered and Garrett escorted him to prison to await trial. It took just a few hours in the courtroom for a judge to find Billy guilty of Brady's murder and sentence him to be hanged. Marked for death, The Kid made his callous and dramatic escape from the Lincoln Courthouse in April 1881 and returned to Fort Sumner.

Billy the Kid must have known that Garrett would come for him at the Fort, but he made no effort to leave the County. He might have been resigned to his fate, or perhaps his fame was beginning to blur his judgement and make him feel invincible. The Kid's name was mentioned in newspaper headlines across the country and several "dime novels" had been published telling exaggerated versions of his life as an outlaw. Billy had read books just like those when he was a youth lounging in Silver City with Sombrero Jack, and he'd enjoyed their fast-paced descriptions of gunfights, robberies and desperadoes. Now he was the leading character and outlaw star in the same books.

Garrett and his men came to Fort Sumner on a baking hot night in July. The sheriff left his horse and two deputies outside a low building and tiptoed inside to question an old friend of The Kid – Pete Maxwell – on The Kid's whereabouts. Garrett thought he could persuade Maxwell to betray The Kid, but as he sat down at the head of his bed a bare-chested figure suddenly stumbled into the dark room.

"Who's there?" the man cried out in Spanish, startled by the shape of Garrett looming out of the dark. The sheriff recognized Billy's voice and lifted his gun.

"Who is it?" Billy asked again and Garrett shot him dead.

A Child of the West

Billy the Kid was buried on July 15, 1881, in a graveyard plot with two of his friends from The Regulators. He was 21 years old. The three men shared a headstone with a single word engraved above their names: PALS.

GUNFIGHT AT THE O.K. CORRAL

"He was no angel ... but he never killed a man who did not richly deserve it."

George Parsons, citizen of Tombstone, Arizona, describing Wyatt Earp

Ike Clanton had been drinking whiskey all night long, muttering curses and spoiling for a fight with his old enemies, the Earp brothers and Doc Holliday. He was still drunk and raging in the dawn light, stalking the streets of Tombstone with a Winchester rifle. US Marshal Virgil Earp tracked Ike down and knocked him to the ground with the butt of his pistol.

"If I'd seen you a second sooner I would have killed you," Ike snapped at him.

Virgil dragged Ike over to the courthouse and went off to find the judge, while Morgan Earp kept an eye on the prisoner. When Wyatt Earp stepped into the room, Ike told him he should get ready for a fight.

"Anywhere, anytime," replied Wyatt, trying to control his fury. Clanton and a gang of his cowboy friends had been goading the Earps for months and Wyatt was in no

mood for any more threats.

When the judge arrived, he fined Ike $25 for carrying firearms inside the town and ordered Virgil to leave Ike's guns at a nearby hotel. Ike would be free to collect them when he was ready to leave town. As Ike sloped out of the courtroom he bumped into his friend, Tom McLaury, who had been hurrying over to see if Ike needed any help dealing with the Earps.

Wyatt stepped into the street. "Are you heeled?" he boomed at Tom, thinking he could see a pistol bulging under the cowboy's coat.

"I'm not scared of a fight – if that's what you're looking for," snarled McLaury.

Wyatt smashed his fist into the side of McLaury's head. He left the stunned cowboy rolling in the dust and went off to buy a cigar – to calm his temper.

A few minutes later, Billy Clanton and Frank McLaury rode into town. They heard the news about their brothers at the first saloon they stopped in. Wyatt watched as the cowboys rushed over to a gun store and started loading their gun belts with cartridges.

Then he went to find Virgil – and Virgil went to find his shotgun – while the gang of cowboys left the shop and walked over to the O.K. Corral.

The gunfight at Tombstone's O.K. Corral is the most famous single event in the story of the Wild West. It is remembered as a showdown between two groups of tough frontier fighters – the good lawmen and the bad cowboys – settling a blood feud with their guns. The battle has been immortalized in over a dozen movies and is usually presented with all the Wild West trimmings.

Two lines of grim-faced men advance towards each other across some open ground at the edge of the desert. Their fingers tremble over the butts of their guns, waiting for a signal to draw and shoot. After a ferocious, drawn-out battle the cowboys lie dead in the sand and the lawmen are cheered as heroes for cleaning up their town.

Gunfight at the O.K. Corral

The real gunfight, on October 26, 1881, was much less straightforward. In fact, it was scrappy and bewildering when compared to the gladiatorial contests of the silver screen. Doc Holliday and the Earps came across their enemies in an empty building lot on a dirt street. They had no plan of action and there was no happy ending for them when the smoke cleared, after thirty seconds of frantic gunplay. But their messy, unscripted struggle with the cowboys is more mesmerizing than any movie showdown. The gunfight was bloody proof that the American West really was lawless and *wild*.

In the late 1800s, Tombstone was a wilderness town, rising out of a sun-scorched desert in southern Arizona. There was only one reason to go there – and that was silver – either dug out of the local mines or teased from the pockets of thirsty miners.

A wandering prospector named Edward Schieffelin had stumbled across the precious metal in 1877, while scouring the hills for gold. Schieffelin had spent years hoping to make a lucky strike and soldiers at a nearby fort had often scolded him for going out alone into the Apache homelands. 'The only rock you're going to find out there is your tombstone,' they warned him.

When Schieffelin discovered a rich vein of silver in the desert, he remembered the soldiers and their jibes and named the place "the Tombstone" after them. A few streets of canvas tents and wooden shacks quickly grew up around the silver mines. Within a year, dollar coins were spinning across the counters of ornate saloons as men like the Earps arrived, hoping like everyone else on the frontier to make a fresh start and a quick fortune.

The Earp brothers were no strangers to life on the Western frontier. James, Virgil, Morgan and Wyatt had all served as stage drivers or temporary deputies in rough Kansas cow towns like Dodge City and Wichita. Virgil and James had fought for the Union in the Civil War and Virgil was a seasoned lawman. When the Earps and their families reached Tombstone, late in 1879, he was the only brother who wore a badge – as a Deputy US Marshal. Virgil's brothers were hoping to invest in property, set up a stagecoach company or try their hands at the card tables to earn a living.

Although Virgil had the badge and the experience, Wyatt is the one people remember as the natural leader of the Earp family and a model of the incorruptible, frontier lawman. With his imposing walrus moustache, fierce stare and quick fists, Wyatt had a quiet authority over other men. But there was another side to his character. In his youth he had come close to taking the outlaw trail.

Wyatt Berry Stapp Earp was born in 1848, in the state of Illinois. He could ride and shoot before he learned to read and write and had his first taste of danger when his father moved the family to

California, hoping to escape the disruption of the Civil War. Wyatt helped to defend his wagon train as it crossed through Indian Territory, trading rifle shots with mounted warriors.

When the Earps tired of farming in California they moved to a small town in Missouri, where Wyatt stood for election as a police constable. He won the post and married a local girl but, before he could settle down to family life, his young wife died suddenly.

Stunned by her death, Wyatt left his job and wandered across the Indian Territory, joining the community of runaways, thieves and adventurers who were drawn to this region beyond the reach of the law. He was accused of fraud and stealing a horse – a hanging crime in many frontier towns. But he never stood trial for these crimes – the charges were either dropped or forgotten by the authorities. Whether or not he did turn to crime in his early twenties, he clearly enjoyed being around dangerous men – and this would be his habit for the rest of his life.

Wyatt rode into Wichita, Kansas in 1874. As a capable gambler and brawler, he was attracted to the saloons and gaming tables of this booming cow town, and was quite at home among one of the roughest crowds in the West. The saloonkeepers of the town quickly noticed that Wyatt rarely touched whiskey and was always ready to break up a fight. He helped them to keep the card tables open, so they didn't object when he joined the Wichita police force the following year.

Fearless in any situation, Wyatt used his fists to flatten troublemakers and rarely drew his gun. He had a fiery temper and would sometimes get into scraps with rival officers, but nobody doubted his honesty. When Wyatt came across a drunk lying in the street one night, he searched him for hidden weapons and discovered a roll of $500 stuffed in the man's coat. The drunk couldn't walk so Wyatt dragged him to the cells and left him to sleep. When the man woke up in the morning he checked his pockets and found his wad of money, safe and sound.

Wyatt left Wichita in 1876, after he was sacked from his post for boxing another lawman in a petty dispute. He moved to an even wilder town – Dodge City – and accepted the job of marshal with an old friend from Indian Territory.

One day, he was helping to clear a gang of rowdy cowboys from a saloon when he heard a voice cry out: "Hey, Marshal, watch your back."

Wyatt heard a shot and turned to see a cowboy, armed with a gun, running for the door. A thin, sickly man was standing at the bar holding a smoking revolver. His name was Doc Holliday and his warning shot had saved Wyatt's life.

Dr. John Henry Holliday was three years younger than Wyatt and a dentist by profession. In many ways he was Earp's opposite – a puny, well-educated and alcoholic dandy from the Southern states who was always starting trouble at the card tables where he gambled his nights away. Holliday was so weak, "he couldn't whip a healthy fifteen-year-old boy in a fight," according to another Dodge lawman – but he was still an exceptionally dangerous man.

The young dentist was dying of tuberculosis – known as consumption in those days. In constant pain and coughing up blood from his diseased lungs, Holliday didn't place any value on his life. As a result, he was reckless and aggressive, and there were even whispers that he had killed several men on his journey across the West.

Doc's illness and bad reputation didn't stop Wyatt from becoming his friend. In this unlikely pairing, both men knew that they could trust each other to the death. When Wyatt went to fight the cowboys at the O.K. Corral, he took his own flesh and blood brothers to back him up – and Doc Holliday.

Wyatt Earp left Dodge City when the town started to, "lose its snap," as he put it to a friend. He didn't want to spend the rest of his life guarding the streets of a cow town and he believed his salary was too low for the risks involved. Wyatt was ambitious and he wanted a share of the profits that came from running stagecoaches or overseeing the gambling and drinking in saloons. When Virgil wrote to him suggesting they try their luck in a new boomtown in Arizona, Wyatt jumped at the chance.

By the time the Earps arrived there, Tombstone had around a thousand citizens, and new shops, hotels and bars were opening every day. Two companies were already running stage coaches around the county, so Wyatt bought some land, which he hoped to mine for silver, and played cards. He was soon in charge of a few card tables and striking deals with the saloon owners for a share of the proceeds.

But this brought him into conflict with a group of men who resented Tombstone's increasing size and political influence in the region. They were a rough collection of ranchers, rustlers and drifters who had lived in the wild country around the town before the town had been built. They were known as The Cowboys.

Gunfight at the O.K. Corral

The rapid progress and development across the West often caused tension between new towns and country people. Most of The Cowboys lived on the fringes of the law, rustling cattle and horses from farmers over the border in Mexico. They would change or conceal any identifying brands – the symbols or letters burned into an animal's skin with a red-hot iron – and sell the livestock to ranchers across Arizona. The last thing they wanted was a strong police force in Tombstone. If there had to be a sheriff in the region, to represent the laws of the county and the state, they wanted to make sure that he was sympathetic to their concerns.

US marshals – like Virgil – were employed by the government to enforce the general rule of law, but sheriffs had to stand in local elections and respect the wishes of the people they served. Although Wyatt was interested in becoming Tombstone's sheriff – and had the backing of many of the town's businessmen – The Cowboys used their votes to elect a man who would leave them alone. He was a former bartender, named John Behan, who disliked Wyatt.

Behan was a weak man, who could do nothing to stop the pressure building between the Cowboys and the resolute Earps. After a stagecoach driver was robbed and murdered in March 1881, Wyatt persuaded – or bribed – a Cowboy rancher named Ike Clanton to reveal the hiding place of the men responsible. Wyatt thought their arrest would make him a strong candidate in the next election for a sheriff, but the secret deal was one of the main reasons behind the gunfight in October that year.

Clanton was a bellowing, irascible man who liked to drink whiskey and throw his weight around. He hated Wyatt for knowing that he'd been an informer and became obsessed with the idea that the Earps would betray him to his old friends. Finally, in a drunken show of force, Clanton insulted Holliday and the Earps and challenged them to fight. When he left the courthouse after his run-in with Virgil Earp, he met his brother, Billy, along with Tom and Frank McClaury. Billy pleaded with Ike to come home to the family ranch, but Ike's blood was boiling. The Cowboys were still arguing about what their next move should be as they walked over to the O.K. Corral.

It was a chilly afternoon in Tombstone that day and Doc Holliday wrapped himself in a thick coat before stepping out onto the boardwalk to look for Wyatt. He found three of the Earps – Virgil, Morgan and Wyatt – holding a quiet conference out in the street. When Wyatt explained what was happening – that the Clantons and the McClaurys were armed and threatening to fight – the dentist immediately volunteered to stand side by side with the Earps.

Virgil gave him his shotgun, instructing him to conceal it under his coat so as not to alarm the people of the town. It was illegal to carry a gun in Tombstone, but Wyatt later testified that Virgil had "deputized" his brothers and Holliday before the battle, giving them limited legal powers including the right to carry firearms and make an arrest.

Sheriff Behan was lounging in a barbershop chair when he heard that trouble was brewing with The Cowboys. He rushed out to find Virgil and asked him what he was planning to do.

"I aim to disarm every one of them," Virgil replied.

Behan pleaded with the Earps not to confront The Cowboys. He promised that he would go down to the Corral himself and urge Clanton and his friends to ride away at once or surrender their weapons. As the senior lawman – and brother – among the Earps, Virgil agreed to the sheriff's request.

While Virgil waited for Behan to return, a man named Fonck rushed over in great agitation and described how Clanton was still cursing and threatening to kill the Earps. Virgil explained calmly that the Cowboys were entitled to carry their guns inside the Corral as it was outside city limits. He had no right to arrest them and was expecting them to leave Tombstone at any moment.

Fonck looked even more dismayed. He informed Virgil that The Cowboys had already left the Corral and were gathering in the street at that very moment. This was the last straw for Holliday and the Earps. They checked that their guns were loaded and started marching towards Clanton and his gang.

Before the Earps and Holliday had begun their march, Behan had caught up with Frank McClaury and asked for his gun. Frank shook his head. He told the sheriff he wouldn't hand over any weapons until the Earps were disarmed. Then Behan paced over to Ike Clanton and patted his coat for guns – but he found none. While Ike fumed and shouted, Behan ordered The Cowboys to move off the street into a vacant lot between two timber buildings. He told them to wait there and promised that he would do his best to disarm the Earps.

Behan's heart must have skipped a beat when he stepped around the corner of the empty lot and saw the Earps and Holliday marching down the street only a few hundred feet away. He immediately ran towards them. "I'm the sheriff here," he protested. "And if you go down there you'll be murdered."

Virgil brushed past him and called out: "I plan to take their guns."

Behan shouted something in response. Wyatt and Virgil thought he cried, "I have disarmed them." But Behan later claimed that what he had actually said was: "I have been down there to disarm them."

It was a dangerous thing to mishear. As they rounded the corner of the vacant lot, the Earps were off their guard and had moved their hands away from their guns. They came face to face with the Clantons, the McClaurys and another Cowboy named Billy Claiborne. The Cowboys were clustered around two horses and at least two of them – Billy Clanton and Frank McClaury – were armed with revolvers. Tom McClaury was scrabbling for a Winchester rifle that was still in its scabbard on one of the horses.

"Boys," shouted Virgil, "I want your guns."

Billy Claiborne moved sideways towards a doorway as the other Cowboys backed deeper into the lot. Both sides had drawn their guns. The Earps and Holliday tiptoed forwards until the two groups were only a few feet apart. Virgil heard the click of a gun hammer being pulled back, priming a revolver to fire. He cried out: "Hold, I don't want that."

Gunfight at the O.K. Corral

Two shots rang out. Billy Clanton and Wyatt had both fired and blood was spurting from a hole in Frank McClaury's stomach. Doc Holliday rushed forwards and pointed his shotgun at Tom McClaury, trying to get a clear shot at the Cowboy as he lunged for the Winchester on his bucking horse. Holliday caught Tom in the chest with a blast that blew him out into the street. Ike Clanton lifted his empty hands into the air and threw himself at Wyatt. "I'm not armed," Ike screamed.

Wyatt pushed him away, yelling: "The fight's started. Get fighting or get away."

Ike Clanton ran for his life, darting through the doorway at the side of the lot and abandoning his friends and his nineteen-year-old brother, Billy, to the deputies' guns. While the injured Tom McClaury tottered into the street, Frank shot Virgil in the leg and the marshal fell to the ground. Billy Clanton gasped as Morgan sent bullets crashing into his chest, wrist and guts. But Billy was tough. He grabbed his gun with his other hand and kept shooting as he slumped against a wall.

Morgan screamed as a bullet tore into his shoulder. Frank McClaury was shooting at him as he made a run for the street with one of the horses, trailing splashes of blood in the dirt. Holliday chased after him, dropping the shotgun and drawing his revolver. But he was too slow. When Frank's horse bolted, the wounded cowboy turned his pistol on Holliday, pointing it straight at Doc's chest.

"Got you now, Doc," said Frank.

"Blaze away," replied Holliday.

Frank shot him, clipping him in the leg. Screaming in pain, Doc lifted his own gun and shot Frank in the chest. The Cowboy sagged to the ground and the fight was over. In less than a minute, both sides had emptied their guns. Three of The Cowboys lay dead or dying and the only man to walk away from the battle unscathed was Wyatt Earp.

As Wyatt checked on his wounded friends, Sheriff Behan walked over and told him that the Earps were under arrest.

"Not by you," Wyatt replied. "You lied to us, Behan, and I won't surrender to you. But don't worry, I'm not leaving town. If it comes to a trial, I'll stand by everything we did, and so will the people of Tombstone."

Wyatt had good reason to think he had the support of the town. The first crowds at the scene of the killings saluted the Earps as heroes and cheered the deaths of a Cowboy gang who had been threatening Virgil and his deputies with murder.

But when the dust settled, people started to ask questions about the legitimacy of the gunfight. Billy Clanton and the McClaurys were wealthy ranchers and horse dealers, not outlaws and killers. Some members of The Cowboy group had warrants out for their arrest – gunslingers like John Ringo – but the dead men were not wanted by the law. Their friends were puzzled by Virgil's choice of Doc Holliday as a deputy, particularly as he and Ike Clanton were sworn enemies.

The mood around town gradually changed and, a few weeks after the gunfight, the Earps and Holliday were arrested and charged with murder.

After listening to all the evidence – including the ravings of Ike Clanton from the witness box – a judge decided that the Earps and Holliday had been defending themselves during the shootout and had a right to use deadly force to stop The Cowboys. He set them free.

But if Wyatt celebrated, it was short-lived. In late December, three men with shotguns ambushed Virgil as he was walking back to his hotel. They blasted him in the left arm and back, and surgeons had to remove large pieces of bone from his wounds.

"Don't worry," Virgil joked with his wife, as he lay bleeding on his bed. "I've still got one arm left to hug you with." To the amazement of his doctors, Virgil survived.

Wyatt was convinced that the shotgun attackers were friends of the Clantons and he wanted revenge. Hours after the shooting, he telegraphed US Marshal, Crawley Drake in Phoenix, Arizona, informing him that Virgil was on his deathbed and other lives were at risk. Drake sent a message back appointing Wyatt as a Deputy US Marshal.

But before Wyatt could track down the men who

had tried to kill his brother, the Earps suffered another disaster. This time, Morgan was shot in the back as he was playing a game of pool in a saloon. He died within minutes and his mystery assassin escaped unidentified into the night.

Morgan's death enraged Wyatt and he set out into the desert on a manhunt that claimed the lives of at least four of The Cowboys – the men he blamed for harming his brothers. He rode at the head of a posse that included Doc Holliday, and justified his vendetta – a quest for vengeance – by claiming that he was carrying out his duties as a Deputy US Marshal.

Most of the men Wyatt killed were outlaws or criminals, but he made no attempt to arrest them or bring them to trial. Several Arizona sheriffs thought Wyatt was acting beyond the law and they issued warrants for his arrest.

Although he always maintained that he had acted legally, Wyatt never returned to Tombstone to stand trial. Once his hunger for revenge was satisfied, he rode out of Arizona with his posse and made his way towards Colorado.

Doc Holliday's illness caught up with him in Colorado and he died in a clinic in 1887. The Earps continued their restless wanderings. Only days after Morgan was gunned down, Virgil and his family sold all their property in Tombstone and moved to California, where Virgil served as a lawman until his death in 1905.

Wyatt's later life was more adventurous. He was something of a celebrity after the gunfight, with a reputation for being cool-headed, determined and deadly. For a decade he ran saloons across the West, gambling and prospecting in a string of mining towns. In the 1890s he found work as a stable manager in San Francisco and acted as a referee in a World Heavyweight boxing contest.

At the turn of the century, he sailed north to Alaska, a new American territory that people were describing as the last frontier. Wyatt had spent his whole life chasing a fortune along the edges of civilization and he couldn't resist joining a rush of prospectors looking for gold in the Klondike region. But, like many others, he came back from the snow-locked wastes of Alaska empty-handed.

Wyatt ended his days living modestly in Los Angeles, trying to sell his life story to movie directors and scriptwriters. He hung around the movie sets, chatting with young actors and technicians who were thrilled to meet a legend of the Old West.

A young stagehand named Marion Morrison was impressed by Earp's politeness, his piercing stare and his physical strength. Some years later, when the young stagehand became a famous movie star specializing in Westerns, he changed his name to John Wayne.

In an interview, Wayne confessed that when he played a lawman in a movie about the Wild West, he based the character on his memories of the elderly Earp. But fame on the movie screen came too late for Wyatt. He died in poverty in 1929, almost fifty years after the bloody shootout on the streets of Tombstone.

GERONIMO AND THE END OF A DREAM

"They made us many promises ... but they only kept one. They promised to take our land, and they took it."

Chief Red Cloud, Sioux warrior

He belonged to the Apache tribe and his people called him Goyathlay, meaning one who yawns. When he was 17, he

became a warrior, killing eagles, bears and mountain lions with his spear and arrows.

Goyathlay loved a girl named Alope. As a warrior, he was allowed to marry, but her father wanted a gift of ponies before he would give his blessing to any marriage. So the young warrior caught a whole herd of ponies and brought them to Alope's teepee. She rode away with him as his bride and in the years to come they had three children.

When he was almost thirty, Goyathlay and his people crossed into Mexico to trade goods and horses with the merchants of a small town. Although they lived in peace with the Mexicans, a group of a few hundred Apaches always made a camp outside a town and posted guards when the men went in to trade.

Goyathlay was returning from town one day, when he met a woman who told him Mexican soldiers had attacked the camp. They had stolen the horses and killed the guards before slaughtering dozens of women and infants. Goyathlay's mother, Alope and his three children were all dead.

When Goyathlay went into battle against the Mexicans who had killed his family, he fought like a wild man. The frightened soldiers cried for help from one of their saints – St. Jerome. Apache warriors heard their screams and started using this name when they spoke of Goyathlay. They changed the sounds of the word to suit their own language and from then on he was known as Geronimo.

For almost 30 years it was a name to be feared across the Wild West.

Geronimo and the End of a Dream

Although Geronimo is remembered for being one of the most warlike and stubborn of the Native American chiefs – the last to surrender to the US army – he enjoyed an idyllic childhood.

He was born in 1829, in the alpine valleys of the region that is now New Mexico. Around 6,000 Apaches roamed the canyons and lush meadows of the area, close to the border with Mexico. Like most of the hundreds of tribes scattered across America, the Apaches had their own language, traditions and beliefs. They lived in groups of a few hundred people – known as sub-tribes – trading and visiting other Apache groups when it suited them.

Geronimo's family of *Be-don-ko-he* Apaches moved with the seasons, following the animals they hunted for food and trading goods at settlements. When they set up a camp for a few months they farmed the land around it. As a child, Geronimo helped to dig and prepare the ground for planting crops of corn, beans, pumpkins and melons. His tribe worked together in large, open fields, sharing the vegetables and fruits they grew. They baked bread from corn flour and brewed their own alcoholic drink, which they called tiswin.

When the warriors went hunting, the women and young children collected nuts, berries and wild turnips. Gathering, growing and preparing their food kept everyone busy and made them feel part of a close community. The worst punishment for anyone judged guilty of a serious crime was to be turned out from the tribe. Alone in the wilderness, these outcasts rarely survived for long.

When he was old enough to ride, Geronimo joined the other boys from his village to hunt rabbits, deer, wild turkeys and buffalo. Of all the beasts Native Americans hunted, the buffalo was the most important to their way of life. For tribes like the Sioux, who lived on the grassy plains, the animal was an essential resource of food and materials. They used its hide to make warm rugs, clothes and shoes, and cured the skin to stretch across the poles of their lodges. Each buffalo provided plenty of meat and warriors could make tools, knives and glue from its bones.

In the early 1800s, there were more than 50 million buffalo ranging in huge herds between Canada and Mexico. Although it's a species of bison, it reminded European naturalists of the water buffalo found in Asia and some parts of Europe. So it quickly became known as the American Buffalo. Soldiers and explorers moving West came across grazing herds of buffalo covering the plains as far as the eye could see.

When the railroad companies began laying rails across the Western prairies, the animals lined the tracks and passengers took pot shots at them from train windows. Tourists from the East started to come out by train on buffalo hunting trips, looking for a taste of Wild West adventure as they blasted their shotguns at the grazing buffalo.

The tribes thought the buffalo herds would wander the plains forever, but they had underestimated the settlers' appetite for killing. Using high-powered rifles, professional hunters like Buffalo Bill could slaughter hundreds of buffalo within a few hours. They killed the animals for their hides and their tongues – considered a delicacy in fine city restaurants.

Great mounds of buffalo bones soon piled up in station yards across the West, ready to be loaded into railway cars and ground into fertilizer. In less than 30 years, hunters had pushed the buffalo to the edge of extinction and the plains tribes had lost a source of food they had relied on for thousands of years.

Geronimo played, farmed and hunted with his friends, enjoying life in his tribe and occasional visits to friendly Apache villages. But his carefree childhood ended abruptly when his father became sick and died.

Geronimo and the End of a Dream

The American tribes had many different burial customs, depending on their beliefs and the terrain they lived in. Plains Indians left their dead out in the open, sewing a corpse in blankets and leaving it to decay in a tree or laid out on high scaffolds – to protect the remains from scavengers. Geronimo's mountain tribe dressed the dead man in his best clothes and placed his body deep in a cave, piling rocks around the entrance. When the cave was closed, Geronimo killed his father's horse and gave away all his belongings, following an Apache tradition that relatives should never profit from the loss of a family member.

After his father's death, Geronimo took on the responsibility of caring for his widowed mother. He became a warrior only a few years later and suffered the devastating blow of the Mexican massacre in 1858.

Although he was not a chief when his loved ones were killed, the leaders of Geronimo's tribe thought he deserved revenge more than anyone else. So they put him in charge of a raiding party made up of men from other friendly Apache tribes.

The warriors crossed into Mexico on foot, covering up to 70km (45 miles) each day. Apaches were well known for their speed across rocky terrain and could easily outpace enemy cavalry patrols. After fighting against the Spanish Conquistadors and their descendents, who had ruled South and Central America for hundreds of years, the Apache had become skilled warriors.

Geronimo and the End of a Dream

Geronimo guided the warriors to the valley where his people had been attacked and the Apaches made camp. That evening, eight Mexicans from the town rode out to negotiate with the raiders. Geronimo ordered his men to kill and scalp the riders, as a warning to the town that they must send for their soldiers and prepare for battle.

Savage as it might seem, many warrior societies scalped their enemies, thinking it was part of the sacred business of war to take a trophy from the dead. Fighting was closely tied to a tribe's religious beliefs. Warriors took a different name when they went on the "warpath" (declared war on their enemies), and often painted their skin and wore special clothes or lucky charms into battle. Taking a scalp proved they had been brave in the eyes of their people and their gods. Apaches cured enemy scalps to preserve them, fixing them to the bridles of their horses and exhibiting them with pride at tribal celebrations.

A few tribes copied the habit of scalping from the same Europeans who had crossed the oceans to civilize them. Colonist leaders on the East Coast sometimes paid cash rewards to settlers for the murder of Native Americans. They insisted on seeing a scalp – or at least a pair of ears – to prove a kill, before handing over any money. In Mexico, town officials who feared Apache attacks hired American mercenaries to serve as scalp hunters. These men prowled the deserts, raiding Apache villages and slaughtering men, women and children in their greed for a reward.

Incredibly, some victims of scalping survived the experience. Warriors would often scalp an enemy as soon as they dropped to the ground – even while they were still alive and struggling. Settlers and soldiers who were scalped could at least wear a wig or hat to disguise their head scars, but Indians who lost their scalps were seen as a disgrace to their families. If they weren't driven out into the wild they were often forced to do all the rough, degrading work within the tribe.

Geronimo's brutal tactics brought hundreds of Mexican soldiers rushing to the town and at dawn the next day they marched out to crush the Apaches. After hours of hard fighting, Geronimo split his forces and led a charge across open ground. When the smoke and dust cleared on the battlefield, Geronimo and three other warriors were the only survivors of the charge.

With all their arrows and spears gone, the Apaches spotted two Mexicans with guns running towards them. The Mexicans shot two of the warriors, raised their swords and chased Geronimo and the other man towards some woods where the rest of the Apaches were hiding.

Geronimo reached the trees and armed himself with a spear. He turned to see the Mexicans cut down the other warrior with their swords. Screaming a war cry, Geronimo hurled his spear and killed one of the soldiers. He took the dead man's sword, wrestled the last soldier to the ground and stabbed him.

Geronimo jumped to his feet, waving the Mexican sword over his head and scouring the battlefield for more soldiers to kill. Then he heard a roar from the woods. The other Apache warriors were paying tribute to his bravery with their war cries. They swarmed out from the trees and asked if he would be war chief of all the Apache people.

In the years following this battle, Geronimo led many raids across the border. He always regarded the Mexicans as his natural enemies. When the United States went to war with Mexico in 1846, his tribe didn't protest against US soldiers marching across their lands. Years after America had won this war Geronimo got to know some of the government surveyors who were charting the lands of New Mexico and Arizona – much of which was new American territory, seized from the Mexicans. The surveyors traded with the Apaches, swapping shirts, knives and dollar bills for the warriors' ponies and fresh game.

Like most tribes, the Apaches were bewildered by paper money and couldn't understand its value to the American colonists. In the early years of contact between Native Americans and Europeans, the tribes thought bank notes were worthless. They passed them to their children, who used the cash to make paper shapes and toys.

Geronimo liked the friendly surveyors, but he was more wary of the bluecoats – cavalry soldiers in blue uniforms – who arrived in the 1860s to patrol the area. After a year of peace with the tribes, army officers tried to arrest an Apache chief named Cochise, thinking he had kidnapped a boy from a family of settlers. They invited the chief and some of his family to a meeting in a large tent at Fort Bowie, Arizona. When the officers ringed the tent with soldiers, Cochise slashed his way through the canvas and escaped on a horse.

In fact, Cochise hadn't been responsible for the kidnapping, but the officers arrested his family and threatened to hang them if the chief didn't bring them the boy. Ignorance, prejudice and misunderstandings were responsible for much of the fighting between tribes and soldiers in the Wild West. With no shared language, beliefs or customs, soldiers and native Americans were suspicious of one another and rarely hesitated to use brute force to get their point across.

When Cochise discovered that the officers had detained his family, he kidnapped four settlers as hostages. When he offered to exchange them for his family, the army refused. So Cochise killed the settlers and, in retaliation, the army executed their prisoners. This tit-for-tat bloodbath led to years of angry disputes between the Apaches and US forces.

Geronimo and other chiefs joined with the enraged Cochise to go on the warpath against the bluecoats but they soon realized they were fighting a losing battle. With their artillery and rapid-fire Gatling guns, US troops were too powerful for the lightly armed Apaches.

Geronimo led his small band of warriors and their

families into the mountains and crossed into Mexico. From there he organized raids against isolated farms and trading posts, avoiding confrontation with any large groups of soldiers. He became famous as a guerilla fighter, striking hard and then slipping away to hide in an uncharted labyrinth of canyons south of the border.

Newspaper writers across Arizona and New Mexico used their editorials to pressure army commanders to catch Geronimo. They blamed his warriors for scores of raids – many of which were actually carried out by other Apache groups.

While stories of his crimes spread across the desert states, terrifying settlers in their isolated ranches, Geronimo's people were growing cold and hungry. Hounded by patrols of Mexican or American soldiers, they could never settle down long enough to plant crops or build strong shelters, and it was too dangerous for them to visit towns to trade. When a hard winter settled over the mountains, Geronimo reluctantly negotiated a peace treaty with the US army and agreed to move his people to a government reservation.

For almost twenty years, Geronimo and his tribe lived peacefully on the Apache reservations in Arizona. They cultivated the land and received monthly rations of beef steers, grain, clothing and other supplies from a reservation agent who was employed by the government to supervise the tribe.

There were no fences or walls around the reservation, so when Geronimo was bored or missed his old, nomadic life he would travel into Mexico or visit other chiefs. It was the agent's job to persuade wandering tribes to stay on the reservations, so Geronimo and his people were never allowed to wander far.

There were some good agents in the government's reservation system, but many others were corrupt and cruel. A whole industry grew up of farmers, ranchers and merchants who supplied the reservations, as well as the soldiers who were stationed nearby to guard the native tribes.

Agents often skimmed money or goods from shipments to the tribes and took bribes from merchants in exchange for contracts. They stirred up trouble, starting fights or provoking native Americans to break out of the reservation, in the hope that the government would panic and send more soldiers to the area – earning more profits for the local suppliers.

In 1883, Geronimo heard a warning that US soldiers were coming to arrest him. Another Apache chief, Mangus-Colorado, had been tortured and murdered while under arrest, and Geronimo was convinced that soldiers were planning to kill him too. He gathered together a few loyal followers and left the reservation, stealing horses and supplies for his escape to Mexico.

For the next two years, Geronimo and his band played a cat and mouse game with the army, hiding out in the mountain canyons they knew so well, raiding villages and scraping a living from the land.

General George Crook finally located Geronimo, using hired Apache scouts, and persuaded the old chief that he wouldn't be harmed if he returned to the San Carlos reservation.

Geronimo followed Crook out of the mountains but he was still suspicious of the army. So he slipped away, along with 30 of his people, before reaching San Carlos. Crook's superior officers in Washington were furious, and ordered another general, Nelson Miles, to capture the runaways. Miles put 5,000 soldiers into the valleys and mountains along the border – a third of the US army's fighting men – but he still relied on Apache scouts to bring Geronimo out of his canyon hideaway, in the last months of 1886.

General Miles told Geronimo that he must give up the warpath and settle on a reservation. In return, Miles promised that Geronimo would be reunited with his family within a few days and would live in comfort with them on land provided by the government. Geronimo agreed to surrender as a prisoner of war and Miles kneeled down to brush a few rocks from a rough piece of ground with the back of his hand.

"All the bad things you've done will be wiped away like this," he said, grandly. "And you will start a new life."

Geronimo didn't see his family for a year. Soldiers locked him in a railway car with other Apache warriors – including some of the scouts who had served the army – and sent him to a reservation in Florida, thousands of miles from the lands he called home. The old chief sawed logs in the Florida swamps and watched his friends die in the humid, sickly climate of the camp. He finally rejoined his family at a reservation in Alabama and a few years later they were moved again to Oklahoma.

Stranded on his reservation, Geronimo spent the rest of his life appealing to the government for permission to return to Arizona, but his requests were never granted. He was only allowed to leave the reservation in 1904, when the army exhibited him as a curiosity at the World's Fair in St. Louis, Missouri. Geronimo sold his autograph for a few cents and posed for pictures with the gaping crowds, an elderly reminder of the previous century's Indian Wars, and a time when tribes lived free in their Wild West homelands. He died on his reservation in 1909.

Although in his later years he was seen by some as a defeated warrior, Geronimo's courage and fighting spirit lingers on in the memory of the American public. In 1940, a group of paratroopers dared each other to prove that they were not scared as they prepared to jump from a plane. One of the men promised he would shout the chief's name without stuttering or trembling, as he launched himself into the void. This stunt caught on with other paratroopers, and has led to the widespread custom of shouting, "Geronimo," before making a leap.

The old chief was born in a wilderness untouched

by progress but lived long enough to witness some of the great technological advances of the 20th century, such as the automobile and early flying machines. He also outlived most of the warriors from the Indian Wars, including the two men who had destroyed Custer's cavalry force at Little Bighorn (see page 42): Crazy Horse and Sitting Bull.

Crazy Horse – who had seen the vision of himself as an invincible warrior – died in 1877, after his starving, beaten people had been driven onto a reservation. A soldier stabbed him in the side with a bayonet as the chief tried to escape from an army guardhouse.

Sitting Bull lasted longer, prowling the Sioux reservations after his people had returned from years of self-imposed exile in Canada. The US forces were never sure how to handle the gruff, veteran fighter. They worried that he would become a martyr and symbol of tribal resistance if they executed him, but they were also concerned about his power on the reservation.

To the amazement of many politicians and journalists, the army gave permission for Sitting Bull to appear in Buffalo Bill's touring Wild West show in 1885. Perhaps the generals were eager to have him sent as far away from the reservation as possible, or they might have hoped that the chief would look like a feeble and vanquished old man to the crowds of spectators?

The show featured a variety of Wild West scenes and activities: a buffalo hunt, an attack on a lonely cabin by mounted warriors and a display of shooting skills by the famous markswoman, Annie Oakley. Buffalo Bill bragged that the show provided a true frontier experience for its audience – and used his own reputation as a scout and "Indian Fighter" to lend authenticity to this claim.

Sitting Bull didn't have a speaking part in the performance. He rode once around the arena, staring fiercely at the ranks of families who had paid a few dollars to be transported to the Great Plains. After four months in the show, he asked to be returned to his reservation at Standing Rock, North Dakota, and refused Buffalo Bill's invitation to join him for a long tour of Europe.

Sitting Bull had good reasons for staying at Standing Rock. He had heard reports that the government was trying to buy up most of the land that had been granted to the Sioux people in a treaty made at Fort Laramie in 1868, and force them to live on smaller reservations. Using all his influence, Sitting Bull tried to persuade his warriors not to sign away the rights to their land – but he failed. In 1889 the Sioux sold their old homelands and Sitting Bull gave up all hope of preserving the Sioux's ancient way of life.

Feeling betrayed by his own kind, Sitting Bull retired to his log cabin at Standing Rock. But he was not the only warrior who dreamed of a return to the glory days of the tribes. A religious frenzy was sweeping through the reservations of the West, as a prophet called Wovoka urged every Native American to join in something called the Ghost Dance.

Wovoka's message to the tribes was based on his interpretation of Christianity. He claimed that he had been sent by God to free the Native Americans and to bring back the buffalo herds and the thousands of dead warriors from the Indian Wars.

To earn their salvation, the tribes must be peaceful and loving, but above all they had to dance. Huge crowds gathered in shuffling circles on the prairies, dancing from dawn until long into the night. Reservation agents panicked as the Native Americans abandoned their crops and farm animals to go to the dances. They feared that Wovoka was trying to start a nationwide uprising. When the Ghost Dance reached Standing

Rock, General Miles assumed Sitting Bull must be responsible for the craze and ordered his arrest.

In December 1890, dozens of Indian Police – former Native American warriors working for the reservation agent – surrounded Sitting Bull's cabin. When they brought him outside, there was a struggle with some of Sitting Bull's supporters. The old chief died with a bullet through his ribs.

There was more tragedy in store for the Sioux nation. In the last days of December that year, a US cavalry force from Custer's old regiment intercepted the Sioux chief, Big Foot, and his people at a place named Wounded Knee creek.

Big Foot had heard that Sitting Bull was dead and decided that his people were in danger on their reservation. But the cavalry officers told the chief he must lead his people back, after handing over all their weapons. One of Big Foot's warriors argued with the soldiers when they tried to confiscate his rifle. He accidentally fired a shot and the soldiers opened up with their heavy guns. When the shooting stopped, almost 300 people from the Sioux tribe lay dead in the snow.

The massacre at Wounded Knee marked the end of the American tribes' resistance to the crushing forces of Manifest Destiny – and a bitter end to the Native American dream.

FOUR COFFINS FOR
THE DALTON GANG

"Of course I'm interested in the money ... but there's the lure of the life in the open, the rides at night, the spice of danger, the mastery over men, the pride of being able to hold a mob at bay – it tingles in my veins. I love it. It is wild adventure. I feel as I imagine the old buccaneers felt when they roved the seas with the black flag at the masthead."

Henry Starr, frontier bandit for 30 years, explaining his choice of career. Starr died on the job – shot during a bank robbery.

They came out of the south, five riders on fine horses. A young girl noticed them pass by on the road into Coffeyville and guessed they were livestock buyers or grain merchants coming to do business in her rich, Kansas town. She didn't think it was out of the ordinary that each man had a Winchester rifle fixed to his saddle and a pair of revolvers at his waist. People went around armed in southern Kansas, ready to hunt or protect themselves from wild beasts. And Coffeyville was just a few miles north of the

Oklahoma border. That country was still lawless in places, a hiding place for outlaws, whiskey smugglers and desperate men.

Only three years earlier, the flat grasslands rolling like a sea below Kansas had been part of Indian Territory. But, in the great Land Rush of 1889, 2,000,000 acres of the Territory were divided up between settlers, as a first step towards making a new state known as Oklahoma.

In April of that year, 40,000 people had lined up along the borders of the Territory, waiting for the start of the Land Rush. A settler could claim over 100 acres and win permanent ownership of their land if they worked it for a *few years. At noon on the appointed day a lone bugle call signalled that the Territory was open for development. A flood of people in wagons, on horses and on foot swept across the plains. New farms and towns were staked out and populated within a few hours.*

The five riders on their way into Coffeyville were not farmers or hard-working merchants. They were the Dalton Gang – train robbers and killers who were about to commit a breathtaking crime. With a posse of lawmen only a day's ride behind them, the gang needed a big haul to finance their escape from America. Coffeyville had two banks that stood close to one another and the Daltons were planning to rob them both in a single daring raid.

By the time they rode into Coffeyville on October 5, 1892, the Daltons had become a notorious gang of criminals. But, only a few years earlier, the three Dalton brothers at the core of the gang had been deputy marshals and peace officers, chasing rustlers and thieves. Lots of young cowboys on the frontier ran wild and got into trouble before settling down to a law-abiding life. But Grat, Emmett and Bob Dalton had chosen a different path. After risking their lives wearing a tin star badge, they decided to become outlaws. They disappeared into Indian Territory to form a gang.

The Daltons had learned by bitter experience about the dangers of serving the law. Their older brother, Frank, had been a marshal for the dreaded magistrate, Isaac Parker – known as "the hanging judge" by criminals across the West. Parker's court was based at Fort Smith in Arkansas, just across the border from Indian Territory. He sent his deputies into the wilderness to bring wanted men back to stand trial – dead or alive.

Parker acted as judge in thousands of cases and sent 79 guilty offenders to the hangman. He was unrepentant about the men he had executed, quipping: "I never hanged a man. The law did." Bandits and outlaw gangs would do anything to avoid appearing in his court and they rarely surrendered without a fight. Frank Dalton was shot dead in 1887, as he tried to serve one of Parker's warrants on a group of gunslingers smuggling whiskey into Indian Territory, where alcohol was prohibited.

Lawmen had other reasons to grumble about their jobs, other than the risk of sudden death. None of them got rich on the low salaries paid by the government and they had to spend weeks alone in rough country, far from their families and the comforts of home. It might have been Bob who was the first of the Daltons to turn to crime. He was the most ambitious, aggressive and forceful of the brothers and he had a gift for persuading his friends to join in his dangerous schemes.

Robert Dalton was born in Missouri, in 1868. Brother Grattan had arrived three years earlier and Emmett was the youngest of the three, born in 1871. Their father had been a gambler, drifter and drinker. He moved his family to a village close to Coffeyville, while his sons were boys, before settling on a ranch in Indian Territory.

The Daltons were always brawling at school and could handle a gun and a horse before they were in their teens. Bob was the most gifted shootist and his weapon of choice was the Winchester reapeating rifle, which he fired from the hip. With its long, grooved barrel, the Winchester was more accurate than a revolver. It could hold fifteen cartridges in a tube under the barrel – compared to a revolver's six shots – and was quickly reloaded by pumping a lever in the shape of a hoop below the trigger.

With its firepower and impressive range, the Winchester was one of the most popular rifles on the frontier and some cowboys dubbed it, "the gun that won the West." Bob's fellow marshals acknowledged his shooting skills and there are stories of him paying a young boy to throw tin cans into the air for target practice. Bob could put three bullets through each tin before it hit the ground.

When Bob told his brothers he had a plan to make some easy money rustling horses, they agreed to follow him. Emmett had worked as a cowboy and the brothers recruited some of his friends from local ranches to bolster the numbers of their gang. These men included 'Black-faced' Charley Bryant, who had a gunpowder stain under the skin of one cheek, 'Bitter Creek' George Newcomb, Bill Powers, Bill Doolin and Dick Broadwell.

From the start, the gang proved to be unlucky and

incompetent bandits. When they sold their herd of rustled horses in Kansas, a posse picked up their trail and chased them into New Mexico. After a botched attempt to rob a saloon, the gang split up and the Daltons crossed through Arizona and into California to visit another brother, Bill. They were accused of robbing their first train in California, in February 1891. The Daltons denied having any part in this raid, but the railroad offered a $3,000 bounty for their arrest and they were forced to flee the state.

Two months later they were stealing horses in Indian Territory again and Bob killed a man from a posse that caught up with them in some woods. When Judge Parker heard reports of the murder, he issued a warrant for Bob's arrest and sent his best marshals to track him down.

With the murder warrant and the California railway reward money still hanging over him, Bob decided he had nothing to lose by committing more serious crimes. In May 1891, his gang held up a train and pocketed around $2,000 – small compensation for being hunted men.

Black-faced Charley was the first of the gang members to be caught and killed. A lone marshal arrested him after he became sick and was recognized as an outlaw by the doctor who was treating him. The lawman bundled Charley onto a train bound for a prison in Wichita, Kansas, but Charley snatched one of the marshal's guns and the two men killed each other in a frenzied shootout.

Charley's death was a stark warning to the gang to change their ways. But they robbed three more trains and killed two bystanders before deciding it was time to quit. Low on funds and pursued by a posse of marshals, Bob said he had a fail-safe scheme that would pay for the gang to start a new life overseas.

When Bob suggested robbing the Coffeyville banks, Grat and Emmett thought their brother must be drunk or crazy. No criminal gang had ever dared to attack two banks at the same time. They would be spread out, unable to communicate with each other and exposed to twice the usual risks of discovery and capture. If this wasn't bad enough, there were dozens of people in Coffeyville who could recognize the Daltons from the days when they lived nearby.

But Bob argued that, for this very reason, nobody would be expecting the gang to strike. The banks stood opposite one another on a main street, only a few yards apart. If the gang split into two teams, it would only take them a few minutes to rob the banks, regroup and ride out together before anyone could raise the alarm. He sweetened his argument by adding that Coffeyville was a wealthy market town. In the early hours of morning trading, each bank would be holding tens of thousands of dollars.

Grat and Emmett finally agreed to the plan – although Emmett later admitted that he was so nervous on the morning of the raid he guzzled a pint of whiskey to calm his nerves. Bill Powers and Dick Broadwell were also persuaded, but the other cowboys in the gang thought it was a reckless idea.

Doolin and 'Bitter Creek' Newcomb stayed in Indian Territory and formed another outlaw gang – the Wild Bunch. They were both shot dead within a few years of the Coffeyville robbery.

Bob took his gang north, after making elaborate plans for the escape from Kansas. He hired an accomplice to meet them with a wagon, spare horses and supplies. The outlaws would travel to San Diego disguised as farmers before slipping away on a ship heading south. Bob's friend kept his end of the deal and was waiting patiently for five riders on the day of the raid – but the Daltons never arrived.

The gang reached the heart of Coffeyville just after 9 a.m. They rode through the bustling streets, heading for a hitching post for horses that Bob had used as a boy, which was close to the Condon Bank. Each man was dusty, long-haired and unshaven after spending weeks in the backcountry, but the Dalton brothers still pulled the collars of their coats high around their faces, hoping that no one in town would be able to identify them. As the riders turned into Coffeyville's 8th Street, Bob saw something that made him curse. Workmen had been digging along the length of the street, making improvements to the walkways.

"The old hitching post is gone," he whispered.

Most outlaw gangs studied the layout of any bank they were planning to raid, walking the surrounding

Four Coffins for the Dalton Gang

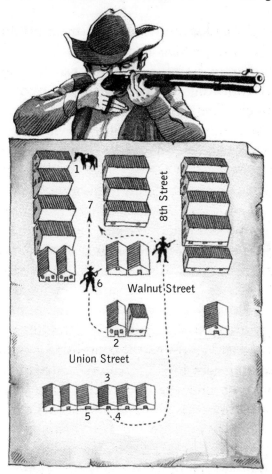

1 - The Dalton Gang hitch their horses and walk down the alley.
2 - Grat, Broadwell and Powers burst into the Condon Bank.
3 - Emmett and Bob raid the First National Bank.
4 - As the citizens open fire, Bob and Emmett exit through the back of the bank, killing Baldwin.
5 - Bob rakes the store with gunfire, killing Cubine and Brown.
6 - Grat and his men run the gauntlet up the alley. Grat kills Marshal Connelly.
7 - The gang are cut down in the alley.

streets and checking each part of their plan for any pitfalls. But the Daltons had been too lazy – or scared – to scout around Coffeyville. Bob was relying on his boyhood knowledge of the town for a place to leave their horses. His hitching post at the corner of 8th Street and Walnut Street had been pulled down weeks earlier.

"Do we call it off?" asked one of the men, nervously.

"No," snapped Bob. "I know another spot."

Bob led his gang into an alley that ran parallel with 8th Street. The far end of the alley opened into Walnut Street, leading to the Condon and the First National banks, but the men tied their horses to a fence at the top of the alley. They were still in sight of Walnut Street, but hundreds of yards further away from their targets than Bob had intended.

This careless choice of hitching place would have fatal consequences for the Dalton Gang. In the days following their raid, the narrow, dirt street where they left their mounts was given a new name: Death Alley.

The gang walked down the alley, pulling their hats down low and gripping their Winchesters. As they came out into Walnut Street, three of the men – Grat, Powers and Broadwell – swung left through the doors of the Condon Bank, leaving Bob and Emmett to cross Union Street and step into the First National Bank.

Aleck McKenna was sweeping the walkway boards outside his shop when he saw the five strangers cross Walnut Street and enter the banks. McKenna recognized one of the men as a Dalton at once – from his build and the rhythm of his walk. He dropped his broom and ran over to the Isham hardware store next to the First National.

In less than a minute, men were running over to the hardware store as news spread that the Daltons were in town. The citizens of Coffeyville began picking shotguns and rifles from the shelves of the store, arming themselves to defend their town.

Inside the Condon Bank, Grat Dalton was menacing one of the clerks with his rifle and stuffing a cotton sack with paper money and silver dollars. While Broadwell and Powers guarded the exits to the street, Grat pushed his way past the clerk. He smiled when he saw that the doors to the bank's vault stood open, stepped into the vault and stared at the safe. Its thick, steel door was shut tight. Grat beckoned to one of the bank's cashiers – a man named Charles Ball.

"Open it," ordered Grat.

"I can't," Ball replied. "Our safe is fitted with a time lock. It's not set to open for another ten minutes."

Ball was a brave man. If Grat had moved forward and tugged on the handle of the safe, the door would have swung open. The time lock had triggered hours earlier and the safe was unlocked.

"We'll wait ten minutes," said Grat.

The words were barely out of his mouth as a shot rang out across the street, like the sound of a branch snapping. A crackle and roar of gunfire started up all around the bank and the battle for Coffeyville began.

The first seconds of shooting must have been bewildering for the five outlaws. They had been in the banks for only a few minutes and had no reason to suspect that the town was rallying to the fight.

Emmett and Bob were the first to come under fire. Their raid had been more successful than Grat's and Emmett was carrying the haul – a sack bulging with $20,000 in paper money and heavy coins – as they hurried out of the bank. A revolver bullet hissed through the air just ahead of them and the two Daltons darted back into the First National's lobby.

After this opening shot, the men at the hardware store opened up with their rifles and shotguns. Dick Broadwell was the first of the gang to be wounded, as a bullet smashed into his left arm. Grat dropped behind the bank counter and heard bullets and shotgun pellets splintering the walls.

"Where's the back door to this place?" Grat growled at one of the clerks.

"We don't have one," answered the man. Like Charles Ball he was lying, trying to prevent the robbers from escaping. The Condon did have a doorway onto the sheltered side of Walnut Street – out of sight of the cluster of shooters in the hardware store – but Grat was too trusting to doubt the man's word.

Bob didn't make the same mistake. He guessed from the steady thunder of shots, breaking glass and cracking wood at the front of the First National, that he was outgunned on Union Street. While Emmett followed with the sack of money, Bob dragged two hostages with him towards the rear of the bank. He stepped through a back door into an alleyway and immediately spotted a young man walking towards him – a store clerk, Lucius Baldwin. Baldwin was holding a revolver in one hand but he thought Bob was a friend of the hostages and was off his guard. Bob lifted his rifle and shot him through the chest.

Emmett and Bob left Baldwin bleeding to death in the alley and hurried around onto 8th Street. As they turned the corner onto Union Street, they could see the ranks of men gathered around the hardware store firing into the Condon Bank. Bob stopped in his tracks and hit the town cobbler, George Cubine, with three shots from his Winchester. A man named Charles Brown ran over to help his dying friend, but Bob shot him dead.

Grat might have seen the men sprawled on the walkway outside the hardware store or perhaps he sensed a lull in the shooting? Whether or not he guessed that Bob was raking the store with rifle fire, he chose this moment to burst out of the Condon and make a dash for the mouth of the alley. Powers and Broadwell sprinted after him, already bleeding from gunshot wounds they had suffered in the bank.

The three men had a long way to run, weighed down with silver dollars and with a dozen guns blasting at them. Grat was hit several times as he bolted towards the alley. Witnesses to the breakout from the bank described seeing clouds of trail dust coming off his long coat each time a bullet struck his body.

Even with the rapid covering fire from Bob's Winchester, Grat, Broadwell and Powers stood little chance of reaching their horses alive. The walkway outside the hardware store had a commanding view straight down the alley and the escaping outlaws were caught in the open.

Grat stumbled sideways and took shelter behind a stairway, but Powers was knocked to the ground by a bullet and killed a few yards from his horse. From his hiding place, Grat watched Marshal Charles Connelly charge across some rough ground and rush into the alley. Grat shot the marshal in the back and made a last sprint for his horse. He made an easy target for Coffeyville's best marksman, John Kloehr, who had just joined the fight. Kloehr shot Grat through the throat and the outlaw spun around and crumpled next to the body of the lawman he had murdered only moments earlier.

Broadwell was luckier. He made it onto his horse before Kloehr put a bullet into him. Even as the life seeped out of his body, Broadwell leaned forward and kicked his horse into action. He was the only member of the gang to make it out of Coffeyville that morning. But Kloehr's aim was true and the outlaw died and fell from his horse only a mile from the edge of town.

While Grat lay bleeding to death in the alley, Bob and Emmett broke away from the fight and hurried up 8th Street looking for a route back to their horses. They followed a narrow passage and came out into the alley, in clear view of the hardware store.

Bob saw the flashes of the guns from Walnut Street and wheeled around to fire, but a shot sent him spinning to the ground. He cocked his Winchester and managed to stand, when a bullet from Kloehr's rifle hit him in the chest. Emmett gasped as a bullet broke his arm and another ripped into his side. He was shot twice more as he lifted himself onto his horse, still cradling the sack of loot in his arms. Instead of galloping to the top of the alley and escaping, Emmett spurred his mount towards Bob. He reached a hand down to help his dying brother, but Bob only whispered: "Ride Emmett – and die game."

It was bold but useless advice. Before Emmett could sit back in his saddle, the town barber, Carey Seaman, blasted him with both barrels of his shotgun. Emmett crashed to the ground next to his brother. His body was peppered with 23 bullet and shotgun pellet holes. Five other men lay dead or dying around him and three other corpses were stretched out on the floor of the hardware store. Coffeyville had battled and beaten the Dalton Gang in one of the bloodiest gun battles in the days of the Wild West.

The Daltons' raid on the town had lasted just over ten minutes. In that time Coffeyville's defenders – most of them farmers or storekeepers – had fired hundreds of rounds into the two banks and along Death Alley. Emmett Dalton was the only survivor from that hailstorm of bullets.

A gang of citizens carried the outlaw to the doctor's office and laid him out on a couch. They put his four dead friends on display, draped across a platform of rough planks, and returned to the doctor's building a few hours later with a length of rope. In their rage, a crowd of the townspeople wanted to lynch Emmett, by hanging him from a tree or telegraph pole.

"There's no need for that," the doctor shouted down to the crowd. "His wounds will do the job for you."

The doctor was wrong, but his gloomy prediction saved Emmett's life. Satisfied that the outlaw would suffer the same fate as his four dead friends and fellow citizens, the mob dispersed. Emmett was still alive in the morning, but by then the town was in mourning and nobody was in the mood for any more killing.

The last member of the Dalton Gang slowly regained his strength and stood trial in 1893. He was sentenced to life in prison and only escaped the gallows because he had been so busy holding the money sack he hadn't fired a single shot during the battle.

After 14 years of imprisonment, Emmett convinced the governor of Kansas that he was a reformed man and won his pardon. He spent the rest of his life trying to sell his story in Hollywood, Los Angeles, writing two books and a series of failed movie scripts.

Before he died, in 1937, Emmett enjoyed telling his version of the botched raid to anyone who would listen. At the end of the tale he always made the same, melancholy observation on the death of his friends and brothers: "Crime never pays."

ALL THE
PRETTY PONIES

"It will probably surprise you to hear from me away down in this country, but U.S. was too small for me. The last two years I was there, I was restless. I wanted to see more of the world."

Butch Cassidy, in a letter to an old friend from his ranch in Argentina

In 1900, Vic Button's father owned the CS Ranch outside the small town of Winnemucca, Nevada. Ten-year-old Button was out riding one morning when he saw some men camping on the ranch and went over to speak to them. One of the men was a stocky, cheerful cowboy who owned a fine, white horse. Button liked the man and over the next few days he visited the camp to listen to his stories and take part in riding races and other games. When Button complimented the cowboy on the speed of his horse the man joked: "Kid, he'll be yours one day."

A week later, the man with the white horse and two of his friends robbed the bank in Winnemucca. They rode out of town firing their revolvers in the air to scare people

off the streets. But Deputy George Rose grabbed his rifle and ran down to the train station.

The bandits were riding along a track that followed the Southern Pacific Railroad for several miles and Rose thought he might be able to catch up with the robbers. He jumped into an engine and roused the driver. Rose was soon leaning out of the train and blasting at the outlaws with his Winchester. But he was too far away and moving too quickly to do any damage.

After a hard ride of thirty miles or so, the outlaws turned off the track and stopped at a remote ranch. The owner of the ranch was waiting with some fresh mounts for the gang. They quickly swapped their saddles over and were ready to go. But, before leaving, the cowboy with the white horse gave some special instructions to the rancher.

"Do you know the boy at the CS place?" he asked.

"I do," replied the man. "That'll be Vic Button."

All the Pretty Ponies

"Well, you make sure Vic gets this horse."

The cowboy had just robbed a bank and come under fire. He must have known that there was a posse already thundering towards him, but he still stopped to keep his promise to a young boy he barely knew.

That cowboy was Robert LeRoy Parker – better known as 'Butch' Cassidy.

The arrival of the horse in North America must rank as one of the greatest advances in the tide of progress across the continent. There were other inventions and tools that helped people to survive on the frontier. Settlers used their guns to hunt and to protect themselves. They bought cast iron stoves for their log cabins, to provide hot food, warmth and a social meeting place through the worst of the winter storms. But the horse allowed explorers, farmers and their families to range deep into the American interior and cover great distances in only a few days.

The railway and, later, the motorcar brought new revolutions in mobility and cross-country trade, but for most of the 1800s a horse was a settler's most valuable possession. When Robert Parker was born in April 1866, some old ranchers still used horses as a form of currency, trading and bartering with the animals instead of using cash. Parker grew up around horses and for most of his life he rode them, traded them – and stole them.

Parker was raised in southern Utah by Mormon parents – members of a church group that had settled in Utah to escape persecution in the eastern cities of America. Life was tough for the Parkers and Robert found work as a ranch hand when he was 13, passing his wages to his mother to help put food on the table. He was still in his teens when he made friends with a cowboy and frontier wanderer who had signed up at the ranch where he was working.

Mike Cassidy struck the young Parker as an exotic and exciting character. He was a gifted horseman, had seen the West and knew how to use a gun. Some of the older men on the ranch whispered that Cassidy was a rustler and a rogue too, but Parker ignored their warnings.

When Cassidy drifted away from Utah, Parker got itchy feet himself and told his family that he was leaving for Telluride, Colorado, to seek work in the town's silver mines. He didn't mention that he would be driving a herd of stolen horses down to Colorado. Following Mike Cassidy's example, the 18-year-old Parker set out on an outlaw adventure that would last for twenty years and take him many thousands of miles away from home.

Robert Parker took a few honest jobs around Telluride while dabbling in rustling and gambling over horse races. But in June 1889 he walked into the town's San Miguel Valley Bank and ordered the cashier to fill a sack with money. Parker and his two accomplices made off with around $20,000, crossing hundreds of miles of rough country on a series of fresh horses.

All the Pretty Ponies

They lost their trackers in a wilderness of canyons, hidden valleys and high peaks known as Robber's Roost. This stretch of uncharted country was dotted with caves and lonely cabins that made it a haven for wanted men. Over the following years, Parker chose Robber's Roost and two other areas of wild country further north for his hideouts: Brown's Hole and the Hole in the Wall. Brown's Hole straddled the state lines between Utah, Colorado and Wyoming.

In those days there was no effective national police force in America and local lawmen had limited powers of arrest in other states. Outlaws flocked to this lawless borderland, knowing that they were unlikely to cross paths with any deputies. The Hole in the Wall was a secret alpine valley in Wyoming, entered by high passes or a narrow gap between sheer cliffs. Bandits guarded the passes and some journalists even suggested that there was an outlaw town hidden behind the cliffs, with stores, houses and even a saloon.

Parker used his share of the loot from the Telluride raid to buy a farm and start trading in horses. It was around this time that he changed his name to George Cassidy – borrowing the surname of his rustler mentor and the first name of a childhood friend. (He picked up the nickname 'Butch' after working as a butcher a few years later.)

With his new title, Cassidy might have been hoping to evade the authorities, but there was no sign that he wanted to abandon crime and make a fresh start. He could never resist roping stray cows and horses from the open range – the unclaimed land which livestock owners used to graze and water their livestock – and in the summer of 1894 he was convicted of keeping stolen horses on his ranch.

Cassidy served 18 months of a two-year sentence in the Wyoming State Penitentiary, but prison didn't reform him. On his release, he rode straight back to Brown's Hole and formed one of the most feared gangs in American history – the Wild Bunch.

The Wild Bunch was the name given to a collection of misfits, rustlers and armed robbers who helped Butch to rob a series of banks and trains around the beginning of the 20th century. They took their name from their habit of "hurrahing" small towns when they were flush with money. Drunk on whiskey, they rode their horses through the streets, shooting their revolvers and playing pranks on local citizens. Butch was a born joker. On one occasion he hitched a team of broncos – the name for untamed horses – to a stagecoach and ordered his men to clamber aboard. Butch fired a few shots and the broncos stampeded through the streets, launching the hooting cowboys into the air.

The Wild Bunch played hard but they were experts at their work. Butch planned his raids meticulously, leaving fresh horses and food at intervals along the gang's escape routes, so they could outpace any posses.

They developed a special technique for robbing trains. One of the gang members would climb aboard a train car at a water stop or quiet station and gradually work his way towards the engine compartment. When the train reached a lonely spot on the prairie, the outlaw whipped out his gun and commanded the driver to halt. The rest of the gang would be camped close to the stopped train and Butch would order the driver to uncouple the baggage car and pull it away from the other cars. If the express company messenger refused to open the sliding wooden doors of the baggage car, Butch used sticks of dynamite to blow the doors off their hinges. He used more dynamite to open iron safes. Cash from a Wild Bunch raid was often singed or blackened, evidence of the explosive force they used in their robberies.

All the Pretty Ponies

After four years of riding with his gang, Butch began to feel the pressure of his restless, fugitive life. The West was changing and Butch knew that he would soon be caught or killed if he continued to rob trains. Special posses of marshals had taken to riding in converted railway cars, waiting for the Wild Bunch to strike. They used telegraph messages and the new telephone network to communicate, rushing to the scene of a raid within hours and bringing a stable-car of fresh horses with them. To make matters worse, the train companies were finally strengthening their baggage cars, fitting them with steel plates and bars, instead of wooden planks.

Robberies were getting tougher and the country itself was changing in ways that made Butch's life harder than before. The open range was almost gone, as farmers and cattle barons threw up miles of cheap, razor-sharp wire fencing across the prairies. Even the old wilderness haunts of the Wild Bunch were being mapped and civilized.

Butch knew it was time to quit. He approached the railway companies and state governors in secret, requesting an amnesty – a pardon from any conviction – if he promised to stop robbing trains. But his talks with the authorities broke down. As pursuing marshals closed in on the Wild Bunch, Butch decided to flee the country. In 1901 he boarded a ship bound for Argentina with one of his closest friends from the gang – Harry Longabaugh, better known as The Sundance Kid.

All the Pretty Ponies

The horizon-spanning grasslands of southern Argentina reminded Butch of the Old West. He bought a ranch with Longabaugh and his partner, Etta Place, and was soon raising horses. But there was a wild streak in Butch Cassidy and he couldn't settle down to life as a farmer.

In December 1905, two Americans robbed the bank at Villa Mercedes and escaped on horseback. The planning and execution of the raid was in the classic Wild Bunch style: a quick and efficient raid followed by a lightning getaway. Pinkerton detectives, who had been searching for Butch on behalf of the American railway companies, heard of the robbery and immediately notified the local authorities that members of the Wild Bunch were possible suspects.

Fearing that they might be arrested if they remained on the ranch, Butch and Longabaugh sold their property and wandered across the Andes mountains into Chile and down into Peru. By 1907, they had arrived in Bolivia and started working at a tin mine, bringing in shipments of supplies and cash for the mine owner. Etta Place had returned to America, leaving Butch and Longabaugh to return to their outlaw life.

In November 1908, two Americans stole a mining company payroll from a messenger and vanished into southern Bolivia. When the outlaws stopped to rest for the night in the small town of San Vicente, the local mayor recognized a brand on their mule and guessed they had stolen the animal from the mining company. He rode out to summon an army patrol that was camped a few miles from the town, bringing back with him a squad of soldiers to question the two Americans.

As the soldiers approached the doorway of the strangers' room, a gunshot rang out and the army captain fell dead to the floor. The other soldiers opened fire with their rifles, killing both the Americans.

In the next few days, the outlaws were buried in a shallow grave and news began to filter out about the robbery and their deaths. When Butch's friends in Wyoming and Utah heard the story, they joked that it was all a clever scheme to convince the Pinkertons that Butch was gone forever. But, when his letters stopped coming and Butch was not sighted for several months, people began to accept that it was in fact he and Longabaugh who had died in San Vicente.

One of the last cowboy outlaws was dead and a new century was changing the way of life across America. It was the end of the frontier and the final days of the Wild West.

Usborne Quicklinks

For links to exciting websites where you can meet notorious outlaws, look through photos of the Old West, discover Native American legends and experience a day in the life of a cowboy, go to the Usborne Quicklinks Website at www.usborne-quicklinks.com and enter the keywords "true stories wild west".

Internet safety

When using the internet, make sure you follow these safety guidelines:

- Ask an adult's permission before using the internet.

- Never give out personal information, such as your name, address or telephone number.

- If a website asks you to type in your name or email address, check with an adult first.

- If you receive an email from someone you don't know, don't reply to it.

TRUE
ESCAPE
STORIES

Paul Dowswell

Finally, the night had come to take a trip to the roof. Morris spent the day beforehand trying to curb his restlessness. What if the way up to the roof was blocked? What if the ventilator motor had been replaced after all? All their painstaking work would be wasted. The 12-year sentence stretched out before him. Then another awful thought occurred. The holes in the wall would be discovered eventually, and that would mean even more years added on to his sentence.

As well as locked doors, high walls and barbed wire, many escaping prisoners also face savage dogs and armed guards who shoot to kill. From Alcatraz to Devil's Island, read the extraordinary tales of people who risked their lives for their freedom.

TRUE STORIES OF HEROES

Paul Dowswell

His blood ran cold and Perevozchenko was seized by panic. He knew that his body was absorbing lethal doses of radiation, but instead of fleeing he stayed to search for his colleague. Peering into the dark through a broken window that overlooked the reactor hall, he could see only a mass of tangled wreckage.

By now he had absorbed so much radiation he felt as if his whole body was on fire. But then he remembered that there were several other men near to the explosion who might be trapped. . .

From firefighters battling with a blazing nuclear reactor to a helicopter rescue team on board a fast-sinking ship, this is an amazingly vivid collection of stories about men and women whose extraordinary courage has captured the imagination of millions.

TRUE
SURVIVAL
STORIES

Paul Dowswell

As he fell through the floor Griffiths instinctively grabbed at the bombsight with both hands, but an immense gust of freezing air sucked the rest of his body out of the aircraft. With the wind and the throb of the Boston's two engines roaring in his ears, he found himself halfway out of the plane, legs and lower body pressed hard against the fuselage. He yelled at the top of his voice: "Geeeerrrooooowwww!!!!", but knew immediately that there was almost no chance his crewmate could hear him.

From shark attacks and blazing airships to exploding spacecraft and sinking submarines, these are real stories of people who have stared death in the face and lived to tell the tale. Find out what separates the living from the dead when catastrophe strikes.

TRUE
SPY
STORIES

Paul Dowswell & Fergus Fleming

"In all your years of fame," Kramer explained delicately, "you have known some of the most powerful men in Europe. Would you consider returning to Paris now to mingle again with these influential gentlemen? And, while you're doing this, might you be able to keep me informed of anything interesting they might say?"

Margaretha looked curious but non-committal.

Kramer went on, "We could pay you well for this — say 24,000 francs."

What are real spies like? Some, like beautiful Mata Hari, are every bit as glamorous as famous fictional agents such as James Bond. But spies usually live shadowy double lives, risking prison, torture and execution for a chance to change history.